Seven Stupid Things People Do to Mess Up Their Lives
(and how not to do them)

DR. BEAU ADAMS

For Kim
The smartest thing I ever did was marry you.

Two things are infinite: the universe and human stupidity;
and I'm not sure about the universe.

--Albert Einstein

I remember the day I almost drowned.

I was a little guy, maybe seven or eight. My parents, my two sisters, and I were visiting friends who had a house on Lake Chatuge, just over the Georgia state line in North Carolina. We were having a picnic at a place near their home called Shooting Creek. They call it a "creek," but Shooting Creek is more like a rushing river, especially at the picnic area, which was at the bottom of a cascading waterfall. Enormous boulders on the sides of the creek created a v-shaped effect of water rushing between the rocks. Signs posted in the park area warned in big red letters: "DANGEROUS RAPIDS. DO NOT GO NEAR THE WATER."

The adults pointed out the signs. "You can play, but do not go near the water," they said.

To a young boy who grew up practically living in the creek behind our house, that restriction was excruciating. Creeks were heaven for me. I wanted to turn over rocks and hunt for salamanders and crawdads.

While the adults were pulling out picnic items, I wandered over to the water.

Though I had no intention of entering the creek, I couldn't resist going to the edge, just to look. It didn't take long to discover that the boulders at the edge of the creek were slick. I slipped and shot right into Shooting Creek. The water was cold and much deeper than it looked. In a split second, I was in up to my chin. My right foot caught a rock, and there I was doing my best not to get swept downstream. The water level was just above my mouth but below my nose, which allowed me to breathe. The problem was, I couldn't shout for help.

My eyes bugged out in desperation. I was able to look over to the bank, where I spotted my dad. He'd seen me slip into the creek and was scanning the water's edge, trying to figure out how to get to me. Then I saw a flash, and I heard a splash. My mom hadn't even thought about it. She'd plunged into the creek, and in an instant had her arms around me. Fighting those rapids, she dragged us to the edge, where my dad pulled us out of the water.

Failing to heed the warnings of my parents and the signs posted around Shooting Creek almost cost me my life, but someone bigger and wiser loved me unconditionally and saved me from my stupidity.

God gave us a book full of warning signs. The Bible is the best-selling book of all time. Why? Because it is filled with the message of unconditional love from someone bigger and wiser, someone who can save us from ourselves.

But the Bible is more than just a big sign with red letters warning us what not to do. It also contains a treasure map that can lead us to the lives we dream about.

Let me ask you something: what if someone offered you a free appointment with the best financial advisor in the whole world? Would you show up for that meeting? Or what if the most famous life coach on the planet offered to personally advise you? Would you take that deal? Of course you would!

There's a book in the Bible full of life advice, and it was written by the wisest (and wealthiest) man who ever lived, King Solomon. It's the book of Proverbs. Proverbs emphasizes wisdom, which is, predictably, the opposite of stupidity. We're about to soak up this wisdom for ourselves. We will meditate on it, let it saturate our hearts, and apply God's principles to keep us from heading down the road of stupidity to our destruction.

Proverbs is God's way of giving us the answers to life's tests. It is a giant sign with arrows and big red letters: "DON'T GO THAT WAY. WALK THIS WAY." *Seven Stupid Things* is a close look at the warning signs in Proverbs.

A staff member came up to me one Sunday after a service and said, "While you were speaking, our daughter looked at her mom and me with a shocked expression on her face and whispered, 'Daddy! Pastor Beau just said the 'S' word!'"

Do you know what the "S" word is?

It's "stupid." I said it in a sermon. And as you may have already guessed, every chapter in this book will contain the word.

Now, the first disclaimer I want to make is I'm not calling anyone stupid. There's a difference between being stupid and doing something stupid, and while I never want to call anyone stupid, I think we would all admit to having done some pretty stupid things. If you can admit it like I can, this book is for you, and we're going to have a good time making our way through it.

Although most of us are probably willing to admit doing dumb things, I can actually look back over my life and point to times when I did things that were almost professionally stupid. I have the ability to take it to a whole new level, so please rest assured this book is written from extensive research and experience. I have reached a point now, however, where I can admit I had certain destructive tendencies. I see how I *chose* to do certain things that resulted in harm to myself and to others. At the time, I even knew God was asking, "Why are you making that choice? Why would you even go there? Don't you see where this leads? Don't you see what will be the result?" In every instance, I chose to ignore God.

I believe you have picked up this book because you are tired of ignoring God's warnings. You are looking for a way to defend against the foolishness.

I have taught these principles not only at Community Bible Church in Stockbridge, Georgia, my home church, but also to church leaders in

England, Wales, India, Portugal, and Brazil. There are some common re-actions I have seen over the years, and one thing I've learned is that there may be times I touch a nerve or two. This does not mean I am being vin-dictive. It doesn't mean someone told me about you, and I wrote a certain section just for you.

You may begin to think, *I don't know if I want to read the next chapter; this material is kind of heavy.* I want you to understand the tone of these chapters is one of pure love. In fact, let me say it right here, right now: I love you. I really do. I may not know you personally, but God's love inspired me to write this book for those who cannot hear these principles in person. Just like my mom dove into Shooting Creek to save me from drowning simply because she loved me, I'm here to help you stay out of dangerous waters.

This kind of love only comes from God's Spirit. It's the kind of love that feels like a parent saying, "I'm warning you not to go here or do this because it's only going to mess things up for you. It's going to ruin the amazing life God intends for you."

Now, as much as your parents, your pastor, or even I may love you, it can't hold a candle to how deeply God loves you. God's love is more cer-tain and more real than anything in this world. And it's the reason you're reading this book right now.

So in the same way that tone of correction appears in Proverbs, you will see it here. This is a tone where God tells us straight up, "Don't do this! Quit messing around with this because it's only going to hurt you. This could ruin your life." Take these teachings from God's Word and re-ceive them with a good attitude. They're intended to improve and protect your life. Let them sink in. Ponder them, and spend time meditating on them. With a humble heart, ask the Lord to help you correct whatever is out of balance with His will.

Are you ready to get started and learn some good stuff? This is going to be an exhilarating ride. Let's jump right in and take a look at the first stupid thing that has the potential to really screw up our lives: *Following the Wrong Crowd.*

1

FOLLOWING THE WRONG CROWD

Tell me with whom you associate,
and I will tell you who you are.

--Johann Wolfgang von Goethe

In 2011, the Federal Bureau of Investigation conducted the National Gang Threat Assessment (NGTA), a massive study on gang activity across the United States. The report included the number of estimated gang members, plus statistics on which gangs were the most violent and the criminal methods they used to make money. Perhaps the most disturbing statistic from the report was the one demonstrating that gang membership in the United States had increased from one million active members in 2009 to 1.4 million in 2011, a forty percent increase in just two years.

I wondered what caused young people to join gangs, and I did a bit of research on the topic. What I found was surprising: these kids don't necessarily want to take part in criminal activity, such as selling drugs or murdering rival gang members. What they wanted was to feel accepted, and that is why they joined gangs. Gangs lure young people with the promise of accepting them for who they are.

I imagine few of us would claim to be an active gang member. Before you write that off, though, let's think about it for a second. It's not only the violent criminal gangs that can suck in young men and women and get them to do things they would not ordinarily do.

Take, for instance, the "gangs" of middle school girls. The drive for acceptance in teenage girls is so powerful they form cliques to decide who's in and who's out. Those considered "out" get ganged up on pretty quickly, and believe me, middle school girls can be a brutal bunch. Whether it's through social media attacks, isolation, or physical violence, they prey on girls deemed to be weaker, and they can do serious damage to anyone who cannot or will not conform to their expectations.

What about the "gang" of uncouth businessmen? These are men who might never individually behave in certain ways, but put them together and suddenly they're scheming. *Hmmm, we an create leverage here, provide a toxic loan there, and if we present it just right, we can take advantage of a whole group of trusting elderly people and steal their life savings.* Most business people would never do such as that on their own, but when they're part of a group, they go with it, even adding their own wickedness. They tell themselves they need to compromise to keep their business networking options open.

Ten years ago, a woman in the neighborhood where my parents live in Florida claimed to have the hottest investment opportunity in town. Fifteen- to twenty-percent returns were what she promised her investors, and people were lining up to give her their money. The only catch was you had to be a personal friend or a friend of a friend to invest in her company. My dad's friends began cashing in retirement accounts to invest with this woman, and they recommended my parents as investors to the woman. It was an exciting day when Dad was offered the opportunity to invest. But when he got the details, my dad decided it wasn't for him.

The business purchased high-interest car loans and re-sold them to investors. It seemed fail-proof because investors were issued promissory notes secured by actual vehicles. But Dad was troubled by the fact the business model preyed on people who were down on their luck by providing car loans at exorbitant interest rates. He thanked his neighbors for recommending him as an investor but decided he couldn't be part of something that took such obvious advantage of the less fortunate.

It was one of the wisest decisions he ever made. In 2010, the FBI served a search warrant on the business because it was suspected to be a giant Ponzi scheme. An investigation revealed the business held only $4 million in collateral against $90 million in investor loans. The woman had been reselling the same car notes to her investors, who, in some cases, lived right down the street from one another. Most investors lost all their money. That woman, whom some have nicknamed Bernie Madoff, Jr., is serving a thirty-year sentence in a Florida prison. My parents are grateful to this day they had the wisdom not to follow that crowd.

But it's not just teenagers or people looking to make a few bucks who fall prey to a gang mentality. Women are another group who sometimes gang up. Even though they're no longer in middle school, a group arbitrarily decides who's in and who's out. The lady considered "out" becomes the topic of gossip when others get together. A group like this can tear a person to shreds without her even knowing it. Being a part of this kind of group feels good at first because a person thinks, *at least I'm not the odd one out.*

What about gangs of the spiritually elite? Back in Jesus' day, they were called Pharisees, and they believed they had it all together. These religious leaders observed minute details of the religious law, so they felt spiritually superior to others, yet they didn't even recognize the Son of God when He showed up. These are the people who say, "We're the super-holy, you can't touch this!" Although we don't call them Pharisees today, they're still in every church, and they're really just another gang.

We could go on all day about these little gangs, but it boils down to everyday people like you and me believing, *Man, if I could be part of this group--if they would accept me—I would be so fulfilled. It would provide what I'm longing for.* You see, it is the desire to be loved and accepted buried deep within us that puts us into a place where we're vulnerable to Satan's manipulation. If we don't know his tactics, it will be easy to ignore our consciences in favor of the illusion of love from one of these gangs. That influence could cause us to do things we would never have done otherwise.

Here's the scary part: seeking acceptance in the wrong way from the wrong people can kill you. Proverbs 1:18 says, "But these people set an ambush for themselves; they are trying to get themselves killed." This wisdom seems counter-intuitive, though, because our herd instinct usually tells us we're safest in a group. Sure, not all groups are bad, but we can see how vulnerability that compels us to do anything for acceptance is a way Satan deceives us and takes us to a place of destruction.

So the first stupid thing we do to mess up our lives is *we follow the wrong crowd.* Proverbs 1:10 says, "My child, if sinners entice you, turn your back on them!" It doesn't get much clearer than that, but let's break that verse down just a bit. First, it indicates sinners *will* entice you. It's merely a question of when, not if, it will happen. Second, it tells you to turn your back on them. Simply put, just turn away.

You see, Satan preys on this need for acceptance. Another way to put it is that he preys on the fear of rejection. No one wants to be the outcast. We don't want to be the one who's left alone, so we'll often go with something our hearts are convicted about because—let's face it—sinners know how to manipulate.

The scripture says they entice us, meaning they draw us in. The only way to get away is to simply turn our backs on them. Don't feel bad about it, either!

As we continue reading in Proverbs 1, verses 11-14, we see this:

> They may say, "Come and join us. Let's hide and kill some-one! Just for fun, let's ambush the innocent! Let's swallow them alive, like the grave; let's swallow them whole, like those who go down to the pit of death. Think of the great things we'll get! We'll fill our houses with all the stuff we take. Come, throw in your lot with us; we'll all share the loot.

What's interesting about this scripture is all of us would say, "If anyone tried to entice me to kill somebody, I'd never go along with it." But when we look under the surface, we see what King Solomon is really saying here, and we realize we're more vulnerable than we think. The enticement is really subtle. It starts off slowly, with these people saying, "We'll accept you if you join our cause. You're finally going to be part of a group. You won't be the outcast anymore; you'll be loved." Pretty soon, it progresses to, "Come on, man, you're part of us now! You represent the group. You can't back out now!" And I promise you, if I put you in just the right circumstances, if you're not rooted and grounded in Jesus, pretty soon after that you'd go along with them when they say, "That guy did this to one of our group. He deserves to die, and we'll take his money, too!"

We may think we would never agree to that, but once we have compromised for acceptance, it's just varying degrees of what we're willing to do from there. Most of us would ultimately do just about anything to be accepted, and that's the hook. That's where Satan gets us, so that's where we have to guard ourselves.

When I was a kid, my grandfather taught me to fish. Man, I enjoyed those times so much. We'd go down to High Falls Lake, just a little southeast of Atlanta, and we'd fish all night long. My grandfather taught me how to properly bait a hook, covering it with as much worm as possible. This is because fish are smarter than most people realize, so if a fish sees that hook, he knows to stay away from it. My grandfather and I would cover the entire hook with a really fat, enticing worm, and we'd drop it in the lake, right under the fishes' noses. The fish would think, *Wow! There's a fat worm that just happened to fall right in front of me. This must be my destiny!* That fish would swallow the worm, and we would reel it in.

Satan uses acceptance in the same way. He covers his hook of destruction really well with the illusion of acceptance. If we bite, we're hooked, and we get reeled in.

Granddad also taught me how to clean a fish, and when I say clean a fish, I don't mean washing it off with some soap and putting it back in the lake. No, I mean taking a knife, cutting of the fish's head, then slitting open the belly and pulling out its guts. It's not very nice for the fish, right? Well, that's a graphic picture of Satan's intentions for you. Just as God has a good plan for your life, Satan's plan is to gut you. He is literally hell-bent on destroying what God loves so dearly. So what can you do to avoid his traps?

In the book of Proverbs, I've identified four steps that are sure to save us from this first stupid thing we do to destroy our lives. First, you must believe God loves you as His child, and He wants what's best for you. If you believe that, you'll understand He provides very specific instructions to guard you from Satan's attacks in this area and his attempts to ruin you. In this next chapter, let's discuss some things we can do to keep from following the wrong crowd.

2

HOW TO AVOID FOLLOWING THE WRONG CROWD

Life is like a dogsled team.
If you ain't the lead dog, the scenery never changes.

--Lewis Grizzard

We recently dropped my daughter off at college for her freshman year. If you've ever dropped your little girl off at college, you know this is not an easy thing to do. When we walked into her dorm room, I went straight over to the windows and made sure they could lock and latch and had the safety bolts on both sides. I made sure nobody was getting through that window.

Next, I checked the doors and made sure they were secured with dead-bolts. Then I made sure the security system was working. Finally, I armed my daughter. I gave her mace and all sorts of stuff with which to defend herself. She was armed for a worst-case scenario. I mean, the girl is *packing* right now, and believe me, only a fool would sneak up on her because, well, let's just say it will be a very painful, if not fatal, experience.

Of course, I made sure my daughter was safe because I love her more than my own life. If Dad can't be there, then Dad will make sure she has everything she could possibly need to keep her safe.

Wouldn't it be silly if my daughter said, "Aw, come on, Dad, you just don't want me to have any fun"? That would be ridiculous! Of course, I want her to have a blast. I want her to have the best life possible, which is why I'm doing all of this. I want her to live a long, healthy life without interference from any idiots, bless their hearts.

It's the wise child who says, "Wow. I have a father who loves me so deeply everything he does is for my good. It's not to stifle me." I'm sure you've guessed this is a metaphor for God's instruction, right? Then let's get started. We have four ways God has provided for us to avoid the trap of following the wrong crowd.

Fear God First

Proverbs 1:7 says, "Fear of the Lord is the foundation of true knowledge, but fools despise wisdom and discipline." Not only does the Bible promise it will make us smart; fearing God is also how we avoid the destruction of following the wrong crowd.

Back in my day, discipline was a lot different from what it is today. I mean, my dad had some forms of discipline that might get a guy arrested in today's world. (I'm kidding. Sort of.) My dad would even say something like, "Son, this is going to hurt me a lot more than it hurts you," and I was thinking, *Yeah, okay, why don't you give me that belt and let's just see?* Boy, did I despise that discipline. But now that I'm older, I realize it was only his tough discipline that kept me off certain paths.

When I was in school, sometimes my buddies would ask me to do some really crazy stuff. I would think to myself, *Are you kidding me? Do you even know my dad? Do you realize what he would do to me if he found out?*

Many of you know what I'm talking about. You know what that fear is. It isn't that you were afraid of your dad. You knew he would do anything for you, but God help you if you did something blatantly wicked. There was a conscious knowledge your dad would follow through on some serious discipline that would leave you hurting for weeks, in one way or another. That right there, my friends, is the fear of God. My dad put the fear of God in me. Simply defined, it's a way of realizing there is nowhere I can go that God isn't there. There's nothing I can do He won't know about.

The fear of God is also realizing that what your Heavenly Father thinks about you matters infinitely more than what anyone else thinks. Too often, we shun the fear of God for the acceptance of the world. We're foolish, despising discipline and trying to pretend God is not there. So many of us have lived this way, and Satan simply uses that to manipulate us, to take us down that road to destruction. But the fear of God changes all of that. When you fear God, you know He is your Heavenly Father, and you know you belong to Him. This knowledge is the beginning of wisdom in your life, and it is the first step to putting you on the right path.

Find Good Counsel
Another way to avoid following the wrong crowd is to *find good counsel.* Proverbs 1:8 says, "My child, listen when you father corrects you. Don't neglect your mother's instruction."

Think back to when you were a child. Did you ever say to yourself, *My parents just don't know anything?* I sure did. I used to think, *There is no way my parents know more than I do about life today. It's a different time, a different era, and they don't have a clue what I'm going through.* Of course, the truth was, they had been here longer and had experienced a lot more in life than I had. God put our parents into our lives for a purpose. He put them there as His representatives, and listening to their instructions as children helped us avoid unnecessary mistakes.

That's true even when we become adults. As young children, most of us innately understand the value of our parents' counsel, but as we get older we often carry with us that immature mindset of believing we know better. We think we have it all figured out, and nobody can give us advice about what's good for us. We fool ourselves into thinking we don't need good counsel, but here's the thing: counsel can determine your day, and it can determine your life.

Proverbs 1:5 says, "A wise man will hear and increase learning, and a man of understanding will attain wise counsel." From whom do you get counsel? Because it is a choice. You are the one who decides from whom you will take advice. Do you choose to listen to the counsel of the Lord? Do you read and practice His Word? Do you ask God to teach you and then listen for His voice? You see, you have to seek the Lord's counsel as a priority—the first thing!—every day because, believe me, you will find bad advice around every corner.

Truett Cathy was the founder of Chick-fil-A, and I was extremely blessed to call him a source of wisdom in my life. In fact, much of his counsel still guides me to this day. During my second year of college, I applied for a job at Chick-fil-A headquarters in Atlanta. They hired me and placed me in shipping and receiving. My daily job was to make sure packages went out to the right places all over the country and then to make sure incoming packages were delivered to the right departments internally. The work was nice, but every once in a while, a phone call would come in, and they would toss me the keys to the giant white Ford LTD with the Chick-fil-A symbol on its doors. My job was to drive to the Atlanta airport, where I would pull up to the curb so Truett could hop in next to me, and I would drive him back to the office.

I was just a young college student, but Truett invested so much in me during those short drives. He always asked how I was doing, and we'd just talk about general stuff, but in the middle of our talks, his wisdom would begin to surface. I'd take in every word, absorbing it and relishing it, and one thing that always stuck out to me was Truett always said everything we do is to glorify God.

There was a huge sign that hung outside Chick-fil-A headquarters. It was a Truett Cathy quote, one he used all the time, and it said, "Do it right the first time, every time." That quote has stuck with me so that to this day, if something breaks at the house and I'm tempted to take the easy route, those words will ring out in my head, "Do it right the first time, every time." That's wisdom I caught from some very Godly counsel. It still helps determine and direct my course, and it will serve me to the day I'm called home to Heaven.

So ask yourself, have you chosen wise counsel? Do you seek out Godly counsel? Do you listen to those who have already walked the Godly way and who know that way? I encourage you to find good counsel because it will save you from following the wrong crowd to destruction.

Choose Your Friends Carefully

Our third step to avoiding the trap of following the wrong crowd is *choosing your friends carefully*. Proverbs 27:17 says, "As iron sharpens iron, so a friend sharpens a friend." I urge you to ask yourself if your friends are sharpening you spiritually. Are they leading you in a good way that will build up your life and make you a better person? Or are they dulling your spiritual senses, leading you farther from Christ and closer to destruction?

Here's an example: have you realized you end up looking like the people you hang around? It just naturally happens. Let's say you buy a motorcycle and you start riding, having fun cruising around. One day you notice some other people riding their motorcycles. You think to yourself, *Wow, that dude has a nice jacket with a big, cool-looking patch*. These guys ride over and complement you on your bike, and they invite you to ride with them on their Sunday breakfast run. You know you should be in church, but you figure one or two Sundays couldn't hurt. Before you know it, you're all leathered up, cruising every Sunday with a biker club badge on your back.

Or maybe some new buddies of yours are fans of a football team you never really had any interest in. They invite you over to watch a game, and when you arrive at your buddy's house, they're all wearing the team's colors. You feel out of place, so you borrow a team jersey from your buddy. When the next home game rolls around, you've already ordered your shirt, pants, and hat and are wearing them in style. Now you're really part of the group. The third time you go to a game, you've painted your face and you're even rolling your belly, jumping around, and freaking out for the cameras.

You begin to look like those you hang out with. Don't get me wrong; I'm not saying don't be friendly to everybody. I'm not saying don't be kind or don't minister to different people, but I am saying choose your friends carefully. Be picky about who you surround yourself with on a daily basis.

This can get tricky for Christians. God wants us to reach out to those who don't know Him, but here's the test: Proverbs 2:20 says, "Follow the steps of good men instead, and stay on the paths of the righteous."

When I was younger, I had a youth minister pull me aside one night to say, "Beau, I'm a little concerned about some of the people you're often hanging out with."

Surprised, I said, "Really, why is that?"

He said, "Well, I know you, I know your heart and your intentions, and I know you want to influence these guys and love on them, to make a difference in their lives."

He paused, then added, "Let me ask you this: suppose I wore a white glove on my hand, and then dipped that glove in a pool of mud."

He had my attention.

"Does the glove become muddy?" he asked. "Or does the mud become glovey?"

I was blown away. It was an interesting way to put it, yet I knew exactly what he meant.

"Be careful who you surround yourself with," he continued. "Because you end up looking like them, and you end up following them, and it's very easy to end up doing things you never thought you would do."

I took his words to heart and slowly removed myself from the company of those guys.

For those of you who are single, or dating, you need to choose your boyfriend or girlfriend even more carefully. I can't tell you how many times I've had a young girl come up to me and say, "Well, Pastor Beau, you know, I'm dating this guy, and he doesn't believe in Jesus Christ, but he's not a bad guy. I just feel if I date him long enough I'll be able to bring him to Jesus." Sadly, it doesn't work that way.

2 Corinthians 6:14 tells us, "Do not be yoked together with unbelievers. For what do righteousness and wickedness have in common? Or what fellowship can light have with darkness?" The word "yoked" in that scripture means to be tied together like oxen pulling a wagon or a plow. The weaker ox will wear the stronger one out in no time, because it is a drag on the strong ox, making his work twice as hard.

Most Christians can quote that scripture by heart, yet it is so tragic how many people have come up to me over the years and said, "Pastor Beau, I wish I had taken that advice. Instead, I got involved with this person, and now I'm in a marriage that's a disaster." That sort of thing happens every day, especially in romantic relationships, because of our desperation for acceptance. Trust God to bring you the right person, and wait in faith. He will do it. But never, ever settle for an ungodly companion. You'll be dragged down, possibly to destruction, before you know it.

Find God's Purpose for Your Life
The final step to avoid following the wrong crowd is to *find God's purpose for your life*. Proverbs 19:1 says, "You can make many plans, but the Lord's purpose will prevail." An interesting analogy, I think, is a GPS navigation system.

Not long ago, my wife, Kim, and I used the GPS on her phone while looking for a Chick-fil-A in a new city. We were cruising down the road and this really sweet ladies' voice said, "Stay straight on this road for half a mile." We were already in the exit lane, so we took the exit. Instantly, we heard the voice say--this time, not quite as sweetly--"Make a legal U-turn and get back onto the highway." We couldn't turn at the one light, so we kept driving, and every intersection we came to, the voice said, "Make a legal U-turn, make a legal U-turn."

I started getting annoyed, like, "Man I'm just trying to get Chick-fil-A, alright? Be quiet."

"U-turn, make a U-turn!" she squawked.

Obviously, she was just trying to get us back on course, and we knew that, but I was hungry, and the hungrier I got, the more annoying her voice sounded.

That's often how the Holy Spirit speaks to us. It starts out as a still, small voice, but if we take a wrong turn, it will get more insistent.

As I've mentioned, God has a purpose and a plan for your life, and His purpose is bigger and more amazing than you could ever imagine. But if you don't know what your destination is, how will you ever get there? God wants to guide you and lead you step by step, and He'll reveal the bigger picture as you grow into it. It's a process because every step He shows you is part of His larger purpose. You need to know that in order to aim for it.

The only way you'll find God's purpose for your life is by spending time with Him. You must get into the Word and pray and listen for His voice. It takes discipline. When you reach that place where you can truly say, "Lord, You call the shots in my life. I want Your Spirit to speak to me and lead me every step of the way," that's when you start gaining some real wisdom.

Even when you commit your life to His purpose, there will be times you find yourself taking a wrong exit by accident. We're not perfect, and God knows that, but He'll let us know very quickly, "Make a U-turn. Get out of there, turn around, this is not what I have planned for you." And know this: while you're choosing God's purpose for your life (because it is a daily choice), there might be hundreds of minor roads that tempt you to take a detour. By following His purpose for your life, you can avoid them. Some of these roads might not be bad roads, and they may not lead to an evil place, but they aren't going to get you to your purpose. They aren't going to take you to the Chick-Fil-A!

Finding God's purpose for your life is so important because you have a very special and unique gift that you need to share with the world. Don't ever let your gifts be squandered. Psalm 37:5 says, "Commit everything you do to the Lord. Trust him, and he will help you." The Lord will bring your greatest dreams to pass, if you can find His purpose for your life and then trust and obey Him in that. I guarantee that finding God's purpose for your life will make your entire walk with God so much easier.

There was a man walking along the beach, and he came upon an old fisherman who had a pail full of crabs.

"You'd better put a cover on that pail, or the crabs will crawl out," the man said to the fisherman.

"Oh, no," said the fisherman. "No need for that. The thing about crabs is, if one crawls up the side and tries to get out, the other crabs reach up and grab him and pull him back down. None of them ever escape, even without a cover on the pail."

Following the wrong crowd is like being a crab in that bucket. Fortunately, Proverbs shows us how to avoid the trap of following the wrong crowd. I encourage you to let these steps sink deep into your heart. Let those scriptures get in your bones. Meditate on them, and they will bring you life and joy. They'll keep you on a path that only winds upward.

3

THINKING WE KNOW IT ALL

*Those who think they know it all have no way of finding out
they don't.*

--Leo Buscaglia

When I was growing up, my dad had certain phrases he used to help steer my life. I'm sure your parents did, too. Those little phrases just seem to stick with you. Sometimes when my sisters and I were fighting, for example, they'd pick on me and I would retaliate. They would start crying, and then I'd be in trouble. Of course, my reaction was always, "That's not fair!"

Without fail, my dad would reply, "Life's not fair!"

I'm sure you've heard that before, but my dad always added a little something to it, like, "Life's not fair, and then you die." I always thought, *Gee, thanks for those words of encouragement, Dad. That really helps.*

Another phrase my dad still uses to this day is, "If you're gonna be dumb, you'd better be tough." That's a good one, isn't it? It's really another way of saying "Stupid hurts." I'm sure we all know from experience stupid hurts, so why do we do stupid things?

In 1912, a magnificent ship was preparing to set sail on her maiden voyage from England to New York. Before the ship cast off, the captain,

Edward Smith, was overheard to say, "Even God Himself could not sink this ship." With its sixteen watertight compartments, this ship was revolutionary. If it were to hit something and even as many as four of those compartments were breached, the ship would still float. There had never been a catastrophe at sea matching that level of disaster, so the captain may have felt justified in believing it was unsinkable. They set sail in confidence, expecting the trip to be nothing less than a lovely, majestic cruise.

Late in the evening on the fourth day of the voyage, as the band played in the first class ballroom, with passengers dancing and enjoying themselves, even the confident crew joined in the revelry. Because of their belief in the ship, they left only one person out on watch, even though they had receive six warnings about sea ice that day. That lone watchman spotted a giant iceberg looming, but the ship was traveling at her maximum speed and was unable to turn quickly enough to avoid it. The great ship sideswiped the frozen mountain of ice. As with all icebergs, three quarters of the ice was below the ocean's surface, so to the eye it didn't look like much. The passengers, most of whom were dancing and celebrating, only felt the ship shudder a bit. They thought it was nothing to be concerned about; the ship was unsinkable! So the band played on. But that iceberg slit open one, two, three, four, then five compartments. The gash was only a quarter of an inch wide, but it was large enough that water began to fill those compartments. Less than three hours later, the ship plunged to the bottom of the sea. Over fifteen hundred people died.

Why did that happen? From the overconfidence of the captain to the lack of additional watchmen, the issue can be traced back to pride.

In this chapter, we're going to look at the second stupid thing we do to mess up our lives, and that is *thinking we know it all*.

I remember as a kid thinking I knew everything about *everything*. Life was just so simple, and it amazed me how adults seemed to complicate matters with their hesitation and thoughtful delays. When I was a little bit older, I looked back and realized I hadn't known as much as I thought. Then in my late teens, I reached the point where I thought, *now I really know it all. I'm practically an adult, and I understand adult decisions, and I know a lot more than the "old fogies."* The funny thing is I look back now and realize I didn't know anything.

The weird thing is most of us will look back and say the same thing, although many of us have at least one particular area in our lives today where we truly believe we have one or two things truly figured out. 1 Corinthians 10:12 warns, however, "If you think you are standing strong, be careful not to fall." I'm not trying to rain on your parade, but those are sobering words, aren't they? In fact, to follow that up, I believe we can more easily fall into the trap of failure in any particular area of life where we think we know it all. That moment we think we know it all is the very moment our ship begins to sink.

There is a scripture that gives us further insight into this problem. Proverbs 3:7 says, "Don't be impressed with your own wisdom. Instead, fear the Lord and turn away from evil." But notice it also offers a solution. That scripture means never be impressed or satisfied with your own wisdom to the point you don't seek counsel from the Lord for every area of your life. That's what fearing the Lord means; it means to respect and honor His counsel, which will cause you to turn away from evil.

How do we get to that place we think we know it all? Again, the answer is simple, and it all comes down to one word: *pride*. Pride is spiritually lethal. If left unchecked, pride will sink your ship because pride will always keep you from getting the help you need. Pride will keep you from searching for one of the most valuable treasures of God, the treasure of wisdom.

Many of us today believe we have a handle on certain situations. A couple married for twenty years might walk into church, and everybody looks at them and thinks, *Wow, what a couple. Everything's beautiful, and everything's wonderful for them. They're so in tune with each other, and they look like they just have it all together.* The couple enjoys the compliments, and they may even believe they are a model couple, until one day one of them shows up to church without the other. It seems odd, but when it happens again the next week, and the next, friends begin to wonder if everything is okay. Suddenly, the truth comes out that the couple is divorcing. What happened? I'm sure many things happened to get the couple to that point, but one thing is certain: at some point, the *appearance* of being the model couple overrode the humility required to seek the help they needed.

This concept applies to children, too; some parents take it for granted that everything's great and their kids are doing well, and they look as if they have a pretty decent handle on this parenting thing. Yet they haven't read the Bible with the family in over a year, and they are in denial their children are beginning to dabble in things of the world. On top of that, they procrastinate in seeking the help they need.

Or maybe we believe we have it together financially. I mean, we think we are making good money, and we sure spend like we're making good money, but what if we sat down, looked at our checking account, and budgeted to plan for the future? Are we really rolling as high as we thought? What if, in fact, the ship is starting to sink and pride is keeping us from getting the help we need? I know this is a little somber, but these words will bring life to you if you receive them. Consider the following scripture:

> Every young man who listens to me and obeys my instruc-
> tions will be given wisdom and good sense. Yes, if you
> want better insight and discernment, and are searching for
> them as you would for lost money or hidden treasure, then
> wisdom will be given you and knowledge of God himself;
> you will soon learn the importance of reverence for the
> Lord and of trusting him. Proverbs 2:1-5

I wonder if there are any treasure hunters reading this book today? Do you want to know what one of the greatest treasures in the world is, one more valuable than gold, silver and precious jewels? It's God's wisdom, because God's wisdom will bring everything you need and more. It's like finding a bottle with a Genie in it who grants three wishes and using one of those wishes to ask for more wishes. Those who hunt for God's wisdom know they desperately need God's Word to keep their ship afloat, so they search for it with everything they have.

Notice the rewards God promises when we do what He says, ". . . Then wisdom will be given you and knowledge of God himself; you will soon learn the importance of reverence for the Lord and of trusting him." In other words, if you search for it with all your heart, if you really want it, God will give you wisdom and all the blessings that follow it. Proverbs 2:6-8 continues:

> For the Lord grants wisdom! From his mouth come knowledge and understanding. He grants a treasure of common sense to the honest. He is a shield to those who walk with integrity. He guards the paths of the just and protects those who are faithful to him.

Are you a desperate treasure hunter? Do you know the value of God's wisdom? Are you intently seeking to grasp the wisdom of God? Are you desperate for it? Because if you are, you will be rewarded. Then again, if you are not intentional about seeking God's wisdom, you will inadvertently be susceptible to the world's foolishness.

Perhaps you found yourself falling back into this mindset of simply absorbing whatever the world sends. You're living on the junk food of life. Stop it! The world is corrupt, and if you passively feed on what the world offers, you'll eventually become what you eat.

What if you walked into your church's auditorium, sat down in your chair, and happened to notice the Bibles in the racks on the seats in front of you had been replaced with smutty magazines? What if, on a Sunday morning, your church played one of those movies you watch after you've sent your kids to bed? And what if, through the sound system that usually plays worship music, your church started playing some of those tunes you've been listening to in the car, on your ride to work? You know the songs I'm talking about, the ones where you think *I shouldn't be listening to that, but I need to be up on pop culture in order to be a good conversationalist. I know the difference between right and wrong, so it's all right!*

What if all that was happening when you walked into church? I know exactly what would happen; you would write a stern note on the feedback cards, you'd send your pastor a very strongly worded email, or you'd make a fiery phone call. You would be disgusted, unable to believe your pastor would allow that stuff in the church. Into *God's house!* Yet we do this every day. 1 Corinthians 3:16 says, "Don't you realize that all of you together are the temple of God and that the Spirit of God lives in you?" Why are we not just as appalled at all the filth we allow in our ears, our eyes, and our minds? We saturate our souls with the world's sewage, and we get so good at explaining it away--*Well, you know, I'm an adult. I know how to filter this out of my brain, and it really doesn't affect me because I've grown beyond all that. It's no big deal.* In our pride we say, "God, I've got this!"

What's so weird is we are surprised when our lives fail in a certain area while we've been filling our minds with worldliness and smut and covetousness. Proverbs 23:7 says, "For as he thinks in his heart, so *is* he..."

We have to ask ourselves, "What do I really want?" Do you want the treasure? Do you really want the rewards found in the Word of God, the wisdom God is willing to pour out on you? If you really want those rewards, then you have to start searching for it. The first step is subduing your pride and submitting to God's Word, because thinking you know it all is diametrically opposed to God's wisdom.

Let's get down to brass tacks: according to God's Word, there are at least three things we can do today to keep us from the trap of thinking we know it all. 1 Peter 5:6 gives us the first answer: "If you will humble yourselves under the mighty hand of God, in his good time he will lift you up." What does it mean to humble ourselves before the Lord? What does that even look like?

Humility is submitting to God's authority; it's going to God and saying, "Okay, Lord, you're right. You're God and I'm not. Your way is the correct way." Humility is acknowledging God knows better than we do, even about our own lives, and then applying His Word in our lives.

The truth is we desperately need God in our lives at all times. It is nothing but pride and arrogance to believe we can do better without God. In fact, it is a trap from the enemy. Pride wants to keep us in our foolishness, but humility is what will cause us to cry out for help. Humility is admitting, "I truly don't know it all, and I'm not going to pretend like I do any longer." Pretending only digs your hole deeper. Humbling yourself under the mighty hand of God is the way out of trouble you may not even know you're in.

What if one day you said to your spouse, "You know what, honey? We're going to quit pretending." What if you reach out and grab your spouse's hand and say, "Let's just get the help we need to keep this boat afloat. Let's make this marriage work or die trying?" What if when you get home today, you call a family meeting and say, "Guys, we've been pretending too long, and it's been a mess, but from this day forward, we're going to seek the Lord in this area of our lives. We're going to go humbly before Him and find the answers and apply them"? That attitude could be the SOS that summons deliverance.

The second thing that keeps us from thinking we know it all is *developing an appetite for God's Word*. Joshua 1:8 tells us, "Constantly remind the people about these laws, and you yourself must think about them every day and every night so that you will be sure to obey all of them. For only then will you succeed." The word "laws" in that verse means the Word of God. If we can only succeed by meditating and feeding our spirit the Word of God, then surely a healthy appetite for God's Word is necessary. But how do you develop an appetite for something you're honestly just not hungry for?

Years ago, my wife was planning dinner and she suggested making Brussels sprouts. I told her straight out, "Honey, we don't do Brussels sprouts in this house." I mean, I don't like big cabbages, so I sure don't like sneaky little cabbages. Well, Kim had this recipe. She pretty much insisted, and I kind of resisted, but you know how that goes, right? I've been married long enough to know which battles are futile.

Kim brought those Brussels sprouts home and cooked those little cabbagey things up with all of the ingredients from her recipe. She brought the dish out, and I was already turning up my nose when she commanded me to try it. I took a hesitant bite, and then, suddenly, my face changed. "Wow, honey!" I said, munching on the little Brussels sprout. "You know, that is not too bad. I could get used to these little things here and there." Kim, being very smart and mindful of our health, made more a couple of weeks later, and guess what? I liked them again! Now, at least once a month, I ask her if she will cook Brussels sprouts.

That's weird, isn't it? I developed an appetite for something that is good for me. I'm sure you get the parallel I'm making. In the same way, when your pastor asks if you're reading God's word, you may say, "Hey, that's not my thing. I just don't have a taste for it. I don't read God's word. I mean, it's enough that I show up to church, right?" Well, what if you started reading a verse from one of your favorite books of the Bible every morning? Start with the Psalms or the book of John. What if you meditated on those verses instead of reading the news about another corrupt politician, another shooting, or another threat from somewhere in the world? What if you rolled that scripture around in your head all day, and then you did it again the next day?

Do you know what will happen? The first day, you'll feel better for having read some good news. The next day, you'll feel a little better again, and then one day, you'll get to a point where you don't know how you used to make it through a day without spending time in God's Word. You'll experience a profound change in your life. You will have joy and perspective like you never had before.

How could that be? Well, if you just humble yourself and accept that God's Word can help you more than you know, you will soon develop a craving for the joy it brings. But if you think you know better, you will never experience the benefits.

You might be wondering what I mean when I suggest meditating on the Word of God. The best way I can explain it is by having you engage in a little meditation exercise. Let's use a well-known verse from Proverbs as an example, Proverbs 3:5, which says, "Trust in the Lord with all your heart, and lean not on your own understanding."

I don't want weird you out, so bear with me for a minute. Take the first part of the first sentence in that verse, *Trust in the Lord*. Now, let's break it down, and think of the first word, *trust*. What does trust look like? Or what does trust not look like? Trust doesn't look stressed out. Trust doesn't look like worry. Trust doesn't look like fear. Trust doesn't look impatient. Trust looks like peace. Trust looks like comfort. Trust looks like *knowing* God will come through, no matter what.

Now look at the next line, *with all your heart*. What is your heart? Your heart is where you hold the things most dear to you. Does it say with all your heart, or with part of your heart? What does trusting the Lord with part of your heart look like? Does it involve holding something back, or perhaps even thinking you have some painful area of your life under control?

The next line is *lean not on your own understanding*. If you're holding back, is it because you're maybe leaning on your own understanding? What if God understands more than you do? Does He see the bigger picture? Could He help? Is He reliable? Does He have your best interests at heart? What if you just trusted Him?

Do you know what happened right there? That was a bit of meditating. Another way to think of it is *spiritual digestion*. I like to be walking outside when I meditate on the Word. I'll take a verse, then mull it over and over and over in my mind. I'll break down the pieces, I'll analyze them, I'll put them back together, and then I'll commit the verse to memory. You, however, might just sit somewhere in a quiet room with everything turned off to meditate. There's no right or wrong way to meditate, as long as you are meditating on God's Word.

Think about it. We all meditate. We do it all day every day. We're thinking about the neighbor who just complained about our dog barking too much and how we should have responded. Or we're rehashing the last argument with our spouse. Those are examples of things we need to let go, and wouldn't it be a good idea to replace it with the words God says about us?

I'll bet what you'll find is meditating on God's Word feels like someone just gave you a great massage! As God talks to you, and you feed yourself on His Word, and He speaks to you through His word, all the anxiety and insecurities flow away. The worries disappear, and you realize very clearly that you are not God, and you really don't want to be God of your problems any longer. He is God, and He does a very good job of it.

He reassures us that He has everything under control, and He will even show us specific ways out of our problems.

That's meditating in God's Word! Soon enough, you'll find yourself starting to crave that Word. You'll develop an appetite for God's Word, and you'll realize how much you *need* it and rely on it. And boy, that's when such great joy occurs, because there is a never-ending supply of depth to feed on every day in the Word. Do it, and I promise your life will just continue to go up and up. That is where Godly peace begins to flood your heart and overtake you so that you can't believe you used to be stressed and worried about things that once dominated your life. Now you're walking in His Word and overcoming and growing every day. Yes, you'll always have problems, but you realize that God will always help you solve your problems, and you never have to stress again. All that peace, joy, and hope come because you've developed an appetite for His Word.

On the other hand, do you know what happens when we don't develop an appetite for God and His Word? We try to satisfy ourselves with things that ultimately starve us body and soul.

One of the lesser-known goddesses in Greek mythology was Limos. There aren't many references to her, but there is one short story about her that is an excellent picture of what the wrong kind of appetites can do to us.

The story begins when Demeter, the goddess of agriculture and abundance, is angered by a king named Erysichthon for cutting down a sacred grove. She sends Limos, also known as Famine, to curse the king with never-ending hunger. Here is Ovid's description of Limos (Famine) from *Metamorphoses*:

> Her hair was coarse, her face sallow, her eyes sunken; her lips crusted and white; her throat scaly with scurf. Her parchment skin revealed the bowels within; beneath her hollow loins jutted her withered hips; her sagging breasts seemed hardly fastened to her ribs; her stomach only a void; her joints wasted and huge, her knees like balls, her ankles grossly swollen.

She sounds lovely, right?

Limos (Famine) does what Demeter bids, sneaking into Erysichthon's room one night as he sleeps and "filling with herself his mouth and throat and lungs and [channeling] through his hollow veins her craving emptiness." After that, the king is driven by incessant hunger that drives him to spend all of his wealth on vast supplies of food that never seem to fill him up. Ultimately, his unquenchable appetite leads him to devour himself.

What I find most interesting about Limos (Famine) is she was known by another name. She was also called Fame.

The Greeks were graphic, no question about it. But isn't that really the choice we're talking about here? We can pursue fame, which results in unquenchable appetites, famine, and ultimately devouring oneself, or we can fill up the empty places with the only thing that really satisfies: God and His Word.

So first we humble ourselves before the Lord. Second, we develop an appetite for His Word. The third thing we do to avoid the trap of thinking we know it all is *we seek to honor the Lord in every area of our lives*. We read Proverbs 3:5 when we practiced meditating on it, but we're going to look at a few more verses from that chapter as well, because they're extremely relevant:

> My son, do not forget my law, but let your heart keep my commands; for length of days and long life and peace they will add to you. Let not mercy and truth forsake you; bind them around your neck, write them on the tablet of your heart, and so find favor and high esteem in the sight of God and man. Trust in the Lord with all your heart, and lean not on your own understanding. In all your ways acknowledge Him, and He shall direct your paths. Proverbs 3:1-6

This scripture promises that when we seek to honor the Lord in every area of our lives, we will find favor in the sight of God and man (Wait! Isn't that the definition of fame?). The next few verses describe all kinds of blessings, from health to abundance to joy and peace. But what does it mean to honor the Lord in every area of our lives? It means we need to look at our lives with a magnifying lens, to see if it they are pleasing to God. If not, we need to ask ourselves what adjustments we can make to align these areas with God's will.

God's Word is His will, so we obviously need to know God's Word. That is why the scripture says not to let mercy and truth get away from you; rather, it uses the word pictures of tying them around your neck and writing God's word on the tablet of your heart to emphasize its importance. When you do this, you are making God and His will the highest priority in your life, and it is guaranteed to bring blessings. In fact, God promises if you acknowledge Him in all your ways, He will personally direct your life's paths. I don't know about you, but for me, that's something worth getting excited about.

So why do we struggle to do something that is so good for us, to acknowledge God in all our ways, so He can direct all of our paths? I believe I know the answer. I would imagine every person reading this book has, in some way, been affected by the terrible disease called cancer. Maybe it was someone you knew in school, perhaps it was someone at work, or maybe it was a loved one. In fact, most people know a little about how cancer works. Simply put, cancer is abnormal cell growth that can potentially spread all over the body and kill the good tissues it invades. When the doctor says someone has a spot of cancer, they know it's not something to ignore. Cancer is something you have to attack; you have to fight it because if you don't deal with it right away, it will spread and will infect other parts of your body. Left unchecked, it will consume you.

I believe pride is cancer of the soul. It might start small, but, boy, it can spread so fast. Left unchecked, pride will begin to grow and attack all areas of our lives, to the point we get all puffed up and say, "God, I don't need you in my life. I've got this." And that is the moment our ship's hull tears; compartments one, two, three, four, and five are cut open. Our ship begins to sink.

I have been married twenty-three years, but I would be a fool to say, "I have this marriage thing figured out." I have a twenty-year-old daughter and a twenty-one-year-old son who are both in college, but I would be a fool to say, "I have this parenting thing figured out." I've been a pastor at Community Bible Church for twenty-seven years, but I would be a fool to say, "I have this pastoring thing figured out." Believe me, more than anything, I want to be the best husband God has called me to be. I want to be the best father I can be, and I want to be the best pastor I can be. I want to be the best in so many different areas, and it's all to honor God. The only way to do that is to say every day, "God, I need Your wisdom poured out on me. I don't want to be someone who is too proud and too puffed up to receive the counsel and wisdom that come from You. I need Your help." The secret to resisting pride is praying this prayer *daily* and meaning it. You must acknowledge the Lord in all your ways, putting Him first in everything. Then He will be able to help you, and make your paths straight. It is a constant fight against the cancer of pride. Humility and submission to God are the only way to win this fight.

I want to ask you to commit to searching for the wisdom of God, as if it is fine treasure, the greatest of all, because it really is. When you do commit to searching for God, you will develop an appetite for His Word. Once you have that daily appetite, you will be able to prioritize and acknowledge God in every area of your life. Then you will be protected from the cancer of pride. That's good news!

That was stupid thing number two, and I hope you gained something from this chapter. When I began applying these three principles to my life, things began to change drastically. I know they will work for you, too.

4

CHOOSING THE PATH OF SEXUAL IMMORALITY

You can't always get what you want.

--The Rolling Stones

I had a dentist appointment not long ago. I anticipated a quick cleaning and checkup followed by a chance to chat a bit with my dentist, who is also my good friend. But after my teeth were cleaned and polished, my buddy looked into my mouth and said, "Uh oh."

It made me nervous. "What?"

"It looks like you're going to need some work done."

"Like what?"

"One of your fillings has cracked, and I think I'm seeing a little bit of decay."

I groaned and said, "I really don't have time for that today."

Dr. Al held up his hand. "You're not going anywhere." Then he whipped out a long needle, stuck it into my mouth and gave me shots in a few different spots. And you know what I did? I sat in his chair until he was finished because I knew he was right.

After the shots set in and my face felt like it was about to fall off, Al pulled out a drill and started grinding away at that tooth. Apparently, my face hadn't actually fallen off because every once in a while, if he hit on one particular nerve, I'd come up out of the chair. He would apologize and keep working, and he kept at it until he got all of the decay and filled the tooth back up. Finally, after his assistant rinsed out my mouth, Al slapped me on the back and said, "Now you're good to go."

As I was walking out of his office, I said, "Thank you, Dr. Al!"

Now, that's kind of weird, isn't it? Who thanks the person who has just caused him pain? But if Dr. Al hadn't insisted on doing what he did, I would have been in much more serious pain down the road. A little bit of pain that day in his office along with some corrective maintenance saved me from a great deal of pain down the road.

As we take a walk through Proverbs chapters five and seven, I can almost promise you there will be a little pain. You might squirm a bit and even come up out of your chair once or twice. But my prayer is that as God touches those nerves, those areas of spiritual decay, He will also heal you, so that as you finish this chapter you will be able to say, "Thank you, Lord, for this teaching that kept me from going to a place of destruction." Trust me, a little pain over the next few minutes might save you a lifetime of agony.

Stupid thing number three we do to mess up our lives is *choosing the path to sexual immorality*. Notice I didn't title this chapter "Following the Path to Sexual Immorality," even though a path is ordinarily something we follow. The first thing to understand is we don't suddenly find ourselves in immorality. It is a path we follow because of a choice we make.

One afternoon in the spring of 1955, a sixty-seven-year-old grandmother from Ohio named Emma Rowena Gatewood told her family—eleven children and twenty-three grandchildren--she was going for a walk. She didn't tell them where she was going because she knew they wouldn't let her go. She left her home wearing a pair of Keds sneakers; over her shoulder was a seventeen-pound handmade denim bag filled with an old Army blanket, a shower curtain, a change of clothes, a water bottle, bouillon cubes, some dried fruits and nuts, and an emergency kit. She had no sleeping bag, no tent, and carried less than $200 with her. The next time her family heard from her, she was 800 miles into the 2,050-mile Appalachian Trail. In September of that year, she became the first woman to hike the Trail and the first person to hike it completely through in a single season. When she reached the end of the trail, atop Maine's Mt. Katahdin, she sang "America, the Beautiful" and then said, "I said I'll do it, and I've done it."

By the end of her hike, she was somewhat of a celebrity. *Sports Illustrated* did a feature story on her. She appeared on the *Today* Show and the *Tonight* Show, known to all as "Grandma Gatewood."

She is also the person credited with saving the Appalachian Trail. When she hiked it in 1955, the Trail was in terrible condition. Markers were missing in many places, causing her to lose her way. In some spots, the Trail even became treacherous. Her vocal criticism of the Trail's lousy maintenance led to its revitalization, and the thousands who hike it every year owe her a debt of gratitude.

I don't know where you are today, but I think many of us might find ourselves in the same situation Grandma Gatewood faced. We're at various mile markers on a path toward sexual immorality and in serious danger of losing our way. For some, the path is headed in a direction that's downright dangerous.

I imagine some of us are at the point where the seduction is getting exciting. It's already playing over and over in our head, something like this: *It's not a big deal. You deserve this. It's what you've always wanted, and it leads to greener pastures.* So you're edging a little further down the path.

I'm here today to be a trail marker, if you will, pointing you to "Go this way!" In some cases, I'm even begging: "Please don't go there. Please turn around while you still can."

Here's a sobering thought: I may be the only one who says this because we live in an age and culture where it's very likely you have people actually cheering you on as you go along that path. Just flip on the television, and without even trying, you can find a show that makes you think immorality is really no big deal. Maybe you even have a colleague at work with whom you've started heading down that road, and you're telling yourself it's harmless. It's just a little flirting; it'll never lead to anything that could ruin your life. Meanwhile, your buddy is telling you to go for it. He or she is cheering you on: "He's so *charming!*" Or "She's so hot!"

Maybe it's even a family member who sees where you're headed, and that person is a little nervous but doesn't want to be the one who tells you to stop. He or she doesn't want to be the bad guy, doesn't relish being the person you suddenly cut out of your life and won't speak to any longer. So that person says, "Do what you've got to do," or merely remains silent. You might even have a lot of support, with people telling you one casual fling won't matter.

I'm talking to the man who thinks a little bit of texting here and there is harmless. I'm talking to the woman who travels for business and thinks because nobody will know, it's okay to have a little Facebook fling. Or maybe you're a young lady who really doesn't want to go that far but you believe you might lose him as a boyfriend. You so desperately want that acceptance. You hope to avoid the terrible loneliness, thinking if you just compromise here, at least you can keep him. Or maybe you're that young, single guy who wants everybody to think he has it all together. She's not a Christian, but she's cute and definitely down, and all your friends are cheering you on.

So I'll be the bad guy. I'm here to tell you, it ends in utter ruin. You're about to step into a trap. Please listen carefully: do not go there. Proverbs 7:21-23 lays it out for us:

> So she seduced him with her pretty speech, her coaxing and her wheedling, until he yielded to her. He couldn't resist her flattery. He followed her as an ox going to the butcher or as a stag that is trapped, waiting to be killed with an arrow through its heart. He was as a bird flying into a snare, not knowing the fate awaiting it there.

Those are some powerful words, aren't they? First, one thing to know about this scripture is the Bible often uses the masculine form, but this text applies to both men and women. (One of the reasons the book of Proverbs personifies adultery and sexual sin in the feminine form is likely due to the Bible's contrast between the irreverent, unfaithful Babylonian archetype and the faithful and holy archetype of the Bride of Christ.) So we would also be correct in reading these verses this way: "He seduced her with his pretty speech and enticed her with his flattery." I guarantee this definitely works both ways.

Regardless of whether you're a man or a woman, it is not a pretty picture. Choosing the path to immorality is like following another person to your own murder. You are walking into a trap that can ultimately kill you. I know these are serious words, but trust me, going down that path is a betrayal; you're being used. The terrifying part is you think you're safe, enjoying the bait, believing it is relatively harmless fun, then suddenly "BOOM!" You've stepped into a trap, and you're struggling and dying in agony.

When I taught this message in my church I took along a prop that vividly depicted the consequences of immorality. The prop I brought to church was a giant rat trap. Notice I didn't say a *mouse* trap. This was a *rat* trap. Those are a little more serious. What happens when you load one of those with a spoonful of irresistible peanut butter? When a big old rat happens by and sniffs the peanut butter, he's cautious at first. He starts looking around. It looks like it's all clear, like he's good to go. The peanut butter smells delicious, and the more he thinks about it, the more he wants it. He gets a little closer, a little closer. Finally, he decides, *You know what? I've come this far and I'm safe. I'm going to go for it. It can only produce something good. It can only produce something that . . .* SNAP! And it's all over.

The imagery is way more effective live because you can see why a mousetrap is not the same as rat trap. A rat trap doesn't really trap anything; it snaps the rat's spine. In the same way, sexual immorality can lead to both physical and spiritual death.

So how do we avoid this trap of stupid thing number three, *choosing the path to immorality?* The first way is to *obtain discernment by learning consequences.* Proverbs 5:1-6 lays it out for us:

> Listen to me, my son! I know what I am saying; *listen!*
> Watch yourself, lest you be indiscreet and betray some vi-
> tal information. For the lips of a prostitute are as sweet as
> honey, and smooth flattery is her stock-in-trade. But af-
> terwards only a bitter conscience is left to you, sharp as a
> double-edged sword. She leads you down to death and hell.
> For she does not know the path to life. She staggers down
> a crooked trail and doesn't even realize where it leads.

Solomon is trying to warn his son here, but remember this can be applied to both men and women. He is *emphatic*, even desperate, like he's saying, "I know it looks good, but let me help you see through all the false prom- ises." Solomon is teaching his son not to trust everything a pretty girl says. And girls, don't just trust everything a good-looking guy says to you. Discernment, which is often simply defined as the ability to decide be- tween truth and error, allows you to say, "Wait a second now, if I trust the Word of God, I can look down to the end and see what really happens." It's almost like having the superpower of being able to see into the future!

So how do we gain discernment? Discernment is gained first by listen- ing to sound advice, then perceiving and understanding and *believing* the consequences. You know, you can often gain discernment from seeing the consequences of other people's poor choices. All of us have watched people choose paths that result in pain and despair. It is easy to see they would never have chosen that path if they could go back in time. I'm say- ing you'd be very wise to take the free lesson in those cases.

If you are a person who values and practices discernment, the Bible says you have wisdom. But what about the person who doesn't learn from others' consequences? Even worse, what about the person who doesn't learn from his or her own consequences? What does the Bible say about that person?

In our home, we're dog people; we have three dogs. We love our dogs, but those dogs do some pretty gross things sometimes. A dog will get sick to its stomach and throw up. That same dog will then walk around after throwing up in the yard, circle back around and go, "Oh, look at that!

Somebody left me a snack." It's disgusting! But did you know the Bible uses it as a word picture? Proverbs 26:11 says, "As a dog returns to his vomit, so a fool repeats his folly." In other words, a person who makes a bad choice, suffers the consequences, and does the same thing again isn't really that much smarter than the family pet.

What about you? Are you a person who learns from consequences in your own life, or even from somebody else's poor choices, and then decides to steer clear of that stupid decision? This actually happened with several of my own family members. They chose a certain path, and I saw the pain going on in each of their lives and the tremendous damage that was done. I remember thinking, *Man, I do not want to go there. God help me never to go there.* You see, James 1:5 says, "God gives wisdom generously to all who ask." God will give us that same discernment to be able to see through the lies, to see through the garbage thrown at us every single day. You can have that discernment to know what the real end is--the true consequence, not what someone is trying to make you believe for his or her own purposes.

Since I've been pastoring, many people have come into my office seeking counseling about poor choices they've made. It's interesting that I have never heard the first person say, "Well, Pastor Beau, to be completely honest, cheating on my wife was the best decision I ever made." It has not happened once. For that matter, I've never had a young man come to me and say, "Pastor Beau, seriously, sleeping around with as many girls as I could was the best decision I ever made. It has made my marriage SO much better." I've never had a young lady come into my office and sit down and say, "Pastor Beau, I was searching for attention, so I gave myself to several guys along the way, and they all lost respect for me and ditched me, but you know what? It was the best decision I ever made, and it has made my life much better." It just doesn't happen because the opposite is true.

I wish you could witness the tears that have been shed in my office, the agony and devastation where person after person has come in and wept uncontrollably, saying, "I wish I could go back and change it all. I've caused so much pain, I've destroyed my home, and my kids won't even talk to me anymore. I wish I could fix it." But in many instances, the damage is irreversible.

Let's consider for a moment some of those irreversible consequences of sexual immorality. In addition to the emotional devastation it wreaks on folks, you could contract hepatitis (did you know a scripture in Proverbs warning against sexual immorality says an arrow will strike your liver?). You might be infected with HIV/AIDS, which, unless God miraculously intervenes, is ultimately a death sentence. Some people turn to suicide because they can't face the pain of losing their family and/or financial ruin, another common outcome in cases of adultery. Some people can't handle the betrayal of infidelity and commit crimes of passion. Addiction counsellors will tell you that addiction kills, but do you know the one addiction just as likely to kill the people around an addict as it is to kill the addict? Sex addiction. These consequences are real, and they happen to undiscerning people *every day*. Please don't let that happen to you.

The first Biblical way to avoid the trap of sexual immorality is *learning discernment through consequences*. The second way is *establishing distance by choosing never to compromise*. Proverbs 5:7-14 says:

> Young men, listen to me, and never forget what I'm about to say: *Run from her! Don't go near her house,* lest you fall to her temptation and lose your honor, and give the remainder of your life to the cruel and merciless, lest strangers obtain your wealth, and you become a slave of foreigners. Lest afterwards you groan in anguish and in shame when syphilis consumes your body, and you say, "Oh, if only I had listened! If only I had not demanded my own way! Oh, why wouldn't I take advice? Why was I so stupid? For now I must face public disgrace."

Can you see the secret in there? The world's culture teaches us there is nothing wrong with taking a look. I mean, truly, how can you not take a look? It's all over television and the Internet. In fact, sex is pretty hard to avoid in our culture. This type of reasoning says you're only guilty when you step through the door. There can't be anything wrong with going near those places in your mind, right?

Wrong. This is how sexual immorality begins.

You see, Satan never whispers, "Hey, you have an appointment to commit adultery tomorrow at twelve noon! Be there, okay?" No, we'd see that coming a mile away. Instead, he says, "You can send an innocent Facebook message. You're just asking if you can 'pray' for her." Yet if you're honest, you know you shouldn't be messaging another man's wife, and you've just opened the door to sexual impropriety.

She responds with "Thanks!" and asks how you've been. She adds she was actually thinking about you the other day for some reason.

Feeling more comfortable, and now a little excited, you respond with "Oh really? What were you thinking?" You even add a smiley-face emoticon.

That is what I call the creep of compromise. We creep in just a little bit closer, then closer and closer, until suddenly SNAP! The rat trap has us, and our lives are changed forever.

The key is to establish distance, or as the scripture so plainly puts it: RUN! Get yourself away from temptation. Put some distance between you and the temptation as quickly as possible, because it can, quite literally, kill you. View sexual temptation as a rattlesnake. As soon as you feel that urge of temptation, realize that is the rattle shaking. You're about to get bitten, so you need to turn around and run.

Consider Billy Graham; he's a man of incredible integrity whose ministry lasted a lifetime without scandal. His ministry endured firmly over the years while the ministries of other pastors and Christian leaders were destroyed by scandal. Why is that? Well, if you read Billy Graham's story, you would know he made decision at the beginning of his ministry; he vowed never to be in a room alone with a woman other than his wife, and he stuck to his decision. Do you see the distance he put between himself and temptation? More importantly, do you see it was a very deliberate *choice*?

Many people will say, "Being in the room alone with another woman is not that big of a deal," but he was smarter than that. He was preemptively running from temptation. This is how you escape sexual immorality; you determine in your heart you're never going to compromise, and you establish distance. This way, you're in no danger of compromise creep.

In the same way, consider one of our fathers in faith, Joseph. He was sold into slavery by his brothers and was subsequently purchased by Potiphar, a rich Egyptian leader. Joseph really had no reason to be loyal to Potiphar, but when Potiphar's wife tried to seduce Joseph, this is what he did:

> She came and grabbed him by the sleeve demanding, "Sleep with me." He tore himself away, but as he did, his jacket slipped off and she was left holding it as he fled from the house. (Genesis 39:12)

Joseph *fled* from the temptation. Even though this is probably one of the most brazen women you'll ever read about, Joseph struggled and pulled away from her grip to the point that his jacket came off and he RAN. He established distance, and he did it fast. For you, it might happen that when you're at the office you can't walk down a particular hallway because that guy or girl's office or cubicle is along that path. Take the long way around. Maybe you're a person who needs to give your spouse complete access to your phone and social media accounts. Or if you're not married yet, maybe when you go on a date, you establish boundaries beforehand. This even includes what you're going to see at the movies, to avoid compromise creep. If that sounds extreme, consider the rattlesnake. Would you rather be bitten or remain safe? The only way to success is to establish distance, by choosing beforehand not to compromise.

Lastly, the third way to avoid the trap of choosing the path to sexual immorality is simply *enjoying God's blessings by living within His boundaries*. Look at what Proverbs 5:15-18 tells us:

> Drink from your own well, my son—be faithful and true
> to your wife. Why should you beget children with women
> of the street? Why share your children with those outside
> your home? Be happy; yes, rejoice in the wife of your youth.

When I taught this message in our church, I showed a video of a young lady who told a heart-breaking story. After some serious issues in childhood, she married a Christian man, believing everything would be pretty rosy from there on. Sadly, she hadn't taken her buried problems before the Lord, and after a while, she became unhappy in her marriage. For various reasons, she felt dead in the marriage, and eventually she made the decision to leave.

Within a week of her separation, she met someone else and began an intimate relationship with him. She hired a lawyer and began the divorce process. She knew God, and she knew better, but her heart just couldn't believe she was worthy of real love. Having added adultery to her problems, she now believed her life was unrecoverable. Nearing the end of her rope, she began attending a new church. As she sat in the back during the services, she found she loved singing along to a song whose lyrics included a line about God making beautiful things from our broken lives. She wondered if God could really make something beautiful from the ashes of her life.

After a while, she heard God tell her to return to her husband, cutting all ties to the other relationship. But she was terrified. She wasn't sure she was ready to live in the presence of God's love, for she had never learned how to deal with the agony of the past. After a long, painful seven months, she finally made the decision to end her affair and chose to trust God's plan. She texted her husband strictly out of obedience, asking if she could return home. Her husband welcomed her home and forgave her. God showed her that His love is always faithful, and when she experienced that kind of forgiveness from God and her husband, she realized it is the unconditional kind of love only possible through God's Spirit.

It took some time, but this woman let go of her fears and the pain from her past so that she no longer chases a fairytale. She has true love-- raw and real and devoted. It is an overcoming love.

Remember, the first way to avoid the trap of immorality is to anticipate the consequences. I think this lady's story demonstrates the consequences of having a skewed picture of what real love is. This distorted perception of love keeps us from seeing the value of watering our own proverbial lawns rather than looking for greener grass elsewhere.

God can and will help you work on your relationship so that you appreciate it, not only as a gift from God, but also because of the work you've put into it. It's like the difference between eating a homegrown tomato—one for which you tilled the soil, planted the seeds, and watered the plant—versus one you picked up at the grocery store. Sure, it tastes better because it's fresher, but you love it more because of all the care you put into growing it.

Enjoy God's blessings by living within His boundaries, and if you're someone who has messed up, consider God's astounding mercy, His amazing grace--*how sweet the sound*--that saves wretches like us. He will restore you, but you must go to Him and be willing to do whatever He asks.

I married my wife in 1993, and we're even more in love than ever before. My wife is my angel on Earth, and there is no way I could do what I do without her. I believe the same is true for her about me. The best decision I've ever made, apart from my relationship with Jesus Christ, is the daily relationship I choose with my wife. It begins with a relationship with Jesus, where I call on Him and say, "Jesus, I need you to help me be the best husband I can be."

What is amazing, though, is God has something just like this for you. Friend, believe me, if you desire that and pursue that, God will bring it to your life. You just have to follow these steps.

If you are married, it is without a doubt God's perfect will that your spouse is the one for you, and you need to work hard at watering your lawn and drinking from your own well.

For those who are unmarried, never settle for something you know isn't God's perfect will. Never settle for sex before marriage, never settle for adultery, never settle for anything less than God's best for you.

The Bible tells us we know what love is because He first loved us. Why not step out of that path that leads to destruction, turn around, and instead chase after the best that God has for you? Be content with what you have, pour your best into your own marriage, and God will bless it more than you can imagine.

5

BECOMING LAZY

We often miss opportunity because it's dressed in overalls and looks like work.

--Thomas Edison

In this chapter, we're going to learn about the fourth stupid thing we do to mess up our lives, and this one's a doozy. Quite simply, *we become lazy.* Now, I know you may be thinking, *Pastor Beau, I'm definitely not lazy. I'm too busy, in fact. There's no way this applies to me.* You might even say, "I work at least sixty hours a week," or, "I volunteer in three different ministries." As soon as we begin to talk about laziness, some people automatically shut off and think this message is for somebody else. But I urge you to stick around; you may be surprised.

I think God would say we all have pockets of laziness, those areas in our lives where we haven't really kept up on the necessary maintenance. Several years ago, I knew a guy who worked about a hundred hours a week. He would tell you all about what he did that week, and you'd quickly realize he had a very stressful job. I thought, *Man, that's the least lazy guy in the world,* but one day, I was talking to him, and he began to tell me about some problems in his family life. In that moment, I realized this man had been extremely lazy at home. He was merely avoiding critical family matters by spending long hours at work.

The book of Proverbs points out some of these pockets of laziness. Let's start our study of them by settling on a working definition of laziness. This isn't necessarily taken from the Bible, but for our purposes, I would define laziness as *leaving important tasks undone*. It may be true that we have many responsibilities, but laziness means neglecting the important things. Some of us can name those areas right now; these are the things we have left hanging out there, to be done some time in the sweet by and by. My prayer today is that we go to God and say, "Lord, can you please help me? Can you help me clear this up? Can you help me become the effective person You want me to be?"

I heard this little poem recently: "Laziness is my weakness/It only brings me sorrow/I know that I should give it up/In fact I will . . . tomorrow." Let's talk about how not to be that person. We'll start by examining the consequences of laziness.

Two Consequences of Laziness

Believe it or not, laziness always harms you. Quite often, we don't connect the two, but laziness will always cause trouble. Now, it may not happen right away. It might take a while to play out, but eventually laziness catches up to you, and it's *scary* when it does. Husbands, if you're lazy in leading your family, in making sure your wife and kids see a strong spiritual example, it may not hurt you today, but at some point, it's going to come back to bite you. If you don't devote the time and effort your family needs from you, at some point you will suffer from that neglect and laziness.

The second consequence of laziness is it also harms others. Your laziness will always affect the people around you. Have you ever been around someone who has neglected something important? Maybe it's somebody in your family, or maybe a friend, but that person's neglect of a certain responsibility has made your life that much more difficult. It's not difficult to see that laziness will harm me, and it will harm others, but for some reason, it's difficult to take responsibility for it.

Proverbs addresses the problem of laziness, of course. In the following passage, Solomon is talking to his son again, warning him: *Don't fall into these traps of laziness. They will harm you. They'll cause you problems and later on, you'll have to deal with these things anyway.* Proverbs 22:13 says, "The lazy man is full of excuses. 'I can't go to work!' he says. 'If I go outside, I might meet a lion in the street and be killed!'

That's pretty interesting, isn't it? He's talking about a person who will make up any kind of excuse. Have you ever been around people who come up with ridiculous excuses? You ask them to do something with you, and they come up with the strangest, most random kind of excuse, something like, "No, my aunt is in town from Mississippi, and I have to, uh, drive her to the world's largest flea market." We can always find an excuse, but Solomon is warning us not to make excuses. When there's a task that needs to be done, don't make up these lame stories. Just get it done.

The next scripture we'll look at it is one of the best verses in the Bible about laziness. Proverbs 19:24 says, "A lazy man buries his hand in the bowl, and will not so much as bring it to his mouth again."

That's over-the-top lazy, wouldn't you agree? This guy is hungry, and he's sitting with a bowl of that good, bold flavor Chex mix in his lap, but he's so slothful he puts his hand in the bowl and won't even lift the snack back to his mouth. Now, I know what you're thinking--*Pastor Beau, that isn't me! I can eat a whole bag of Chex mix and my hand is coming back to my mouth every time!*" But I wonder if there are areas in your life where God already has everything set up for you. He's already made every conceivable opportunity available for you to succeed, yet you are too lazy to take that opportunity and run with it. I don't mean to step on any toes, because I'm stepping on my own, too, but that's God's honest truth, and I have to tell the truth so we can all be set free.

I believe God looks into our lives and says, "I have it all laid out for you right here. Just take it and make it yours." But you know what I do sometimes? I just let it sit there. I miss out on experiencing some of the most wonderful things God has for me because I'm too lazy to pursue them. A common example is when God puts a special desire in your heart. Maybe it's a desire to serve special needs kids, and for a number of years, you've thought about doing that. You've put your hand in the bowl, but it's still there. And because it is still in the bowl, all of that joy and all those rewards you could be experiencing are just sitting there going to waste.

Maybe it's a friendship from thirty years ago that God keeps leading you to rekindle. You think, *I'd love to spend some time with that person again*, but you leave your hand in the bowl. God might have even let that person cross your path in the grocery store, and you had the opportunity to invite him or her to lunch, but you left your hand in the bowl.

God has given us these incredible opportunities, yet we get lazy, and we just won't take what He's already given to us. I think sometimes because God's grace is abundant and His mercies are new every day, we tend to abuse that mercy and we are lazy *because* the Lord is longsuffering.

So how do we fix the laziness problem? Like we've seen with the other examples of stupid things we do, the bottom line is we need to seek wisdom. If we're ever going to combat laziness, we must begin with God's Word. God has already given us what we need to get it done, so let's take a look at these scriptures.

Proverbs 10:4 says, "Lazy hands make for poverty, but diligent hands bring wealth." This where we get down to brass tacks regarding laziness. Solomon gives us a contrast here, beginning with what he calls "lazy hands." Solomon tells us these lazy hands lead straight to poverty. Then he follows that with ". . . diligent hands bring wealth." The people with diligent hands, the kind of people who say, "I want to take care of what I need to right now," are what I call "do-it-now" people. Do-it-now people are those who never make excuses and never procrastinate. God says, "Go," and they get it done.

My grandfather was one of those people. In fact, he was so on top of things, he paid his bills the same day they came in the mail. He also refused to mail in a payment he could pay in person. A few years ago, my younger sister was staying with him during a January snowstorm. The mail came, and in it was the bill for his car tag. He was ninety years old, and the roads were treacherous, yet he got in his car and drove to the Clayton County tag office to pay his bill.

I'll bet it wouldn't surprise you if I told you that, even though he was not a wealthy man, he left this life having zero debt and a perfect credit score. That's what happens when you're a do-it-now person.

The next verse, Proverbs 10:5, says, "He who gathers crops in summer is a prudent son, but he who sleeps during harvest is a disgraceful son." What Solomon is saying here is that a prudent—or wise—son begins gathering the crops the minute they are ripe. He doesn't put it off; he gets ahead of the curve. The disgraceful son, by contrast, sleeps through the early harvest in late summer, and he sleeps all the way through the fall harvest. The lazy son is a disgrace to his parents; they are completely ashamed of him. What kind of person wants his parents to be ashamed of him? I sure don't.

So as we begin to look at solutions for laziness, and we study how to have diligent hands, my prayer for us is, *God, help us to develop diligent hands. Help us to never have idle or lazy hands. Give us diligent do-it-now hands instead.* Because it's exciting to have diligent hands! It's rewarding when there is a God-given task to undertake and, instead of procrastinating, we are obedient and step up to it and see it through. Let's become do-it-now people and change our lives in the process.

I think there are three ways to develop diligence; I call these the ABCs of do-it-now people.

The ABC's of Do-It-Now People: Accept the Task

We all have a task or two that we have been putting off. Maybe it's weeding the flower beds or renewing a driver's license or taking homemade chocolate chip cookies to the new neighbors and inviting them to church. These tasks are things you know God wants you to accomplish, but you've yet to leave the starting blocks. For Christians, there has to come a time where we drive a stake in the ground and say, "God, I'm going to do it! I'm moving forward in obedience."

When I say "drive a stake into the ground," what I mean is there were times in the Old Testament when the nation of Israel would put up monuments at certain places after God had shown Himself faithful. These monuments served to remind the Israelites that the Lord was with them always, and He was faithful to help and guide them toward their eternal destiny. I challenge you today to drive a stake in the ground, setting up a monument that says in effect, *God, I know You're faithful. I know You have a great reward for me after this task, and I know You can help me with what's going on here. There will be no more neglect. There will be no more procrastination, no more excuses. Lord, I don't want lazy hands. I want diligent hands. I accept the task.*

I truly hope you prayed that prayer from your heart. And it may have really stirred you up, but how would you walk this out in your daily life? Well, let's say, for example, you see an old friend dressed in rags, sitting at a stop light with a cardboard sign, and he's half-starved. You wave, and you might even say a quick prayer he gets enough money from begging for new clothes and food. "I'm rooting for you, bro!" you shout, and give him the thumbs up. Then you just drive off without giving him a dime.

Where would that get you? Nowhere. You've got to put you faith on display by *doing something* (James 2:14-17).

There is a specific incident that comes to mind when I think about accepting the task. God placed upon my buddy Drew's heart to start a ministry called *Impact Fulton*. On his drive to work in Atlanta every day, he would see homeless people, prostitutes, and drug addicts sitting along the side of the road. God impressed on him to begin to minister to these people who had become practically invisible. Well, Drew is a do-it-now guy, so he was obedient. He took action, and before we knew it, *Impact Fulton* launched with over a hundred volunteers touching lives all around the city.

One night I took my kids to participate in one of these outreaches; it was like a big party thrown for these folks, with all sorts of care and food available to them. I really wanted my children to see what it means to love and serve the destitute. It was so great to see my son, Chase, in the food line helping serve the hotdogs. I was passing out water, while my daughter, Madison, was helping with the meeting. The whole event went really well. When it was time to leave, Chase, Madison, and I had gotten about fifty yards away when we heard gut-wrenching screams coming from one of the parking lots. Now, you have to understand we were in a pretty rough part of town, so my first instinct was to get out of there fast. But when I looked toward the parking lot, I saw a woman sitting on a curb screaming in agony while a man stood behind her, holding both of her hands and looking panicked.

I hurried over see what was going on. I'd never seen anything like it before; the lady's feet were twisted up, almost to the point of deformity, as she writhed in agony. I asked what was wrong. The gentleman with her said, "She's cramping! She's cramping terribly!"

I told Chase and Madison to run back and find some Gatorade or salt or something that might help alleviate the cramps. They ran off, and I was standing there wondering what else to do. The man holding her hands said, "Why don't you grab her feet, and we'll try to straighten them?"

Now, to be completely honest, I don't like feet. Feet are really not my thing. They gross me out. But still in the spirit of helping out, I was like, "Um, okay." So I got down and hesitantly grabbed her feet and started trying, pretty unsuccessfully, to straighten them. She just kept on writhing and screaming in pain, but then she started groaning, "I just want to go to the party!"

By this time, a crowd had started to gather around. One guy standing there suggested, "How about we pray?"

Kicking myself for not doing it sooner, I said, "That's a great idea." So while I still held her feet and the other gentleman held her hands, a group gathered around and put their hands on her, and we started to pray. Almost immediately, her feet started releasing and straightening out. I was in total awe. After a few moments, she was feeling great relief, and everyone started praising the Lord. We lifted her to her feet, and the crowd walked her back to the party.

Now *that* is called accepting the task. That is how you and I can be the gift of God to other people. Some of us will be water-fetchers, some of us will be prayer warriors, and some of us will be foot-holders. The reason we're on this Earth is to get as many people as we can to the party (Luke 14:23 says, "Then the master told his servant, 'Go out to the roads and country lanes and compel them to come in, so that my house will be full'"). But we have to accept the task. We must realize we are responsible for our faith, and our faith operates through our *actions*.

Several years ago, some of my buddies and I were on a flight to Salt Lake City that hit some severe turbulence. The plane started bouncing around in the air, and I don't know about you, but I get really nervous when that starts to happen. My palms got sweaty, and I was white-knuckling the armrest to the point I thought I was going to rip it right off.

I looked around, and everybody was terrified, which made me even more nervous! Then the flight attendant picked up the microphone and said, "Ladies and gentleman, as you know, we are experiencing a little turbulence on this flight, but there is no need to worry because we actually have a preacher onboard." When I heard that, I thought, *Well, that's good! I could use a pastor's prayers right now!* Then I realized she meant ME! One of my buddies had told her I was a pastor, so everyone on the plane was nodding and smiling at me as if my presence on the plane was a good thing. Meanwhile I was thinking, *Oh man! You have no idea! I'm as scared as you are.* Sometimes God puts us in situations so we have an opportunity to step up our game.

The ABC's of Do-It-Now People: Believe God is With You

Joseph is a father of faith in the Old Testament that I constantly go back to when I need a spiritual boost. I read Joseph's story because, first of all, there are many lessons to learn from his life. But there's also one specific dynamic that shows up constantly in his life, whether he's at the top or at the bottom. If you remember, Joseph knew he was destined for greatness very early in life. Being the youngest, he was especially loved by his dad, and God gave Joseph a dream depicting his entire family bowing down to him. Basically, he dreamed he would one day become a great ruler.

If you know the story, you know Joseph, perhaps naively, told his family about his vision. You know his brothers threw him into a pit and sold him into slavery soon after that. Joseph lived as a slave for almost two decades in Egypt, but because God's hand was on his life, he eventually became second in command over the entire empire. In fact, his governance and wisdom far outshone the Pharaoh's. So Joseph had seen it all and he'd been through it all, but in every area of his life, you'll find these words in relation to Joseph: "And God was with him." In every phase of his life, God's presence with Joseph is what stands out.

The lesson, of course, is that God is always with us. In fact, in the New Testament, the Holy Spirit came down from Heaven to live within us and fulfill God's promise that He will never leave us nor forsake us. God never kicks us out of the nest, saying, "You'd better learn to fly pretty fast!" No, He is with us every step of the way. When we confess the sins of those areas we've become a little lazy in and accept the task the Lord has given us, God is with us, right within us. He is our partner. I love what D.L. Moody once said: "If you partner with God, make your plans big!" Even if you don't know where to start, just accept the task. God's grace will provide the ability and knowledge once you step forward in faith. Believe me. Trust me. Try it.

The ABC's of Do-It-Now People: Confidently Move Forward

I love to watch confident Christians in action. These are the people who have experienced God's grace and have really been through the fire. They've been to the mountaintop and through the depths of the valley, yet because they've come out the other side victorious, they have a supernatural confidence.

For some reason, however, there's often a tendency for us to look at that confidence and say, "That person is fake and self-absorbed." We always seem to want to throw some negativity their way, like we need to bring them down to our lazy level a bit. But they're doing it right. They know that with God we can be confident. With God, we can and should be bold. In the early days of the Church, Christians fought tooth and nail to survive. They fought with every fiber of their being to accomplish the mission God had called them to. They faced opposition every day of their lives, yet throughout the early Church we see boldness and courage everywhere. These guys would address kings, saying, "I compel you to accept Jesus as your Savior." They would be imprisoned where their lives could've been snuffed out in an instant, yet they were confident God would save them.

The challenge for you and me today is to take on the confidence of God. We must put on God's boldness like a cloak. We must accept the task. When we believe God is with us, we can be supremely bold and confident! One of the greatest questions I've ever heard is this: "What would you do today if you were fully confident God was with you?" Think about how many things we're apprehensive about moving forward with. But if we truly believe God is with us, what would we do? I believe when we grasp that God is with us in everything we do, we will move forward and never again allow those lazy hands to control us. We will become enthusiastic and diligent, knowing we cannot fail. Before we know it, we'll be changing this world for Him. God's party would fill up rapidly.

Do you know how to do all of that? It's easy, and it only takes two words. Two of the greatest words a Christian can say are: "Yes, Lord." *That's it.* One of the hardest things for me to do is to bow to somebody else's wishes, yet the two most effective words I could ever say to the Lord are simply, "Yes, Lord." Once we obey, God can move. You see, our obedience shows God we're serious, that we're ready to get rid of the lazy hands and put on the diligent hands. Once we're done with the games, God can begin to work with us.

In conclusion, I want you to know that any time God commands something, He always models it for us at some point. This is really encouraging news!

Philippians 1:6 says, "Being confident of this, that he who began a good work in you will carry it on to completion until the day of Christ Jesus."

Unto when? *Completion.* When God begins to work in us, He does not stop until it's completed. The message for you and me today is if we take the steps to put on those diligent hands, desiring to be committed to the Lord and to finish our tasks, God will be sure to complete the work He started.

Think about the last three words Jesus said. These three words are some of the most powerful words ever spoken in human history. In John 19:30, when Jesus was hanging on the cross and was about to die, He said three simple words: "It is finished." Right there, He modeled victory for us. Don't you want to be able to say that? "Lord, I ditched the lazy hands, put on the diligent hands and Lord, I finished my tasks. *It is finished*, Lord." My prayer for you—and for myself--is that God would help us to have diligent hands and that we would say, *Whatever it takes, I accept the task. I believe You, God, and I am moving forward in boldness and confidence.*

Friend, it's go-time. Whatever God has brought up in your heart as you read this today, it's time to get started doing. Maybe it's a relationship issue you need to deal with, yet you've been making excuses. Maybe you've always wanted to have a spiritual influence in your workplace, but you've put it off for far too long, not grabbing hold of the confidence that God is with you. Maybe it's a ministry that you feel God pulling you toward, one you've pushed it off for too long. *Today* is the day you accept the task, and your hands become diligent hands. You can do it. You can change your life today.

6

OVERSPENDING AND INCURRING DEBT

Debt is dumb. Cash is king.

--Dave Ramsey

Americans love to buy stuff. I was curious about what propels this materialism, so I did a little research. I found a study by TNS Global explaining why people enjoy buying. What is interesting is there are some legitimate psychological benefits to purchasing goods.

The study showed we feel more successful when we purchase things. When we go shopping and buy something, it makes us believe we're moving forward in life. Shopping makes us feel better about ourselves.

Researchers also discovered that purchasing goods is relaxing. It's an escape from the stresses of everyday life. Even if you're just window-shopping, imagining yourself on a beach wearing the sunglasses the mannequin is wearing is a form of daydreaming. It's an easy way to feel good about your life for a few moments.

Shopping also provides a strong social connection. Being out and about allows us to run into old friends and even meet new people.

Finally, shopping gives us something to talk about. Guys, how many of you have ever bought a car and then talked about it for three months? I know I have. Ladies, maybe you bought a new dress, and when your friend complimented it, that started a conversation about where you bought it and the great sale you found. There's clearly a social connection to shopping.

But while shopping might be psychologically beneficial at times, the trouble starts when it becomes a crutch. In extreme cases, it can even become an addiction. The positive feelings you get from buying something new and exciting become an issue when you grow dependent on buying material stuff just for the psychological reward. This is where we move from working hard so that we can buy and enjoy what we need to buying things we don't need, often on credit.

The fifth stupid thing we do to mess up our lives is *overspend and incur debt*.

Sadly, this has become a large part of American culture. Living with debt simply isn't the norm in most countries around the world, even in other first-world nations. Debt is an American thing, and the culture of debt in our country is so widely accepted that a 2015 study by Nerdwallet. com revealed the average American household has $130,922 in debt, with $15,762 of that on credit cards. This means when you remove mortgage and car payments, average American families carry over $15,000 of what we call "bad debt." This is debt that cannot easily be repaid at the end of each month, costing a significant amount of money in fees and interest.

Although the number of Americans carrying debt signifies most of us are in this boat, this is still a personal topic. It's personal for me, and I realize that, for some, it might be an incredibly sensitive topic. Debt affects relationships, it affects marriages, and it affects lives. I frequently talk to people who say, "Pastor Beau, I'm right on the edge of financial ruin. One more thing and I'll go over the edge." It seems like every week I hear from someone who says, "I'm going to lose my home. I don't know what else to do. This is the end of the line for me." It's an epidemic, and I want to let you know I completely understand the sensitivity here. Still, it's a real problem.

So how do we figure a way out of our problems? Just like with our other stupid mistakes, we go to God's word to search for instructions. The answer is that God absolutely has a plan for your finances. As Christians, it's critical we come to the place where we ask, "Lord, what is your will in the area of finances? How can I make my financial life pleasing to you?"

Let's start with the realization that debt is not your friend but your foe. Debt is a burden God never intended for us to carry. Proverbs 22:7 says, "Just as the rich rule the poor, so the borrower is servant to the lender." This was written thousands of years ago, yet those words are still accurate today. Look at the second half of that verse: "the borrower is servant to lender." Do you feel like a slave to your debt? Do you sometimes feel like you owe your soul to your credit card company?

I have good news. There's freedom in Christ. It is God's plan for your life to be free of debt, but it requires commitment. Escaping debt doesn't happen in a day because, for most of us, debt has become like a nasty in-law that moved in and now goes everywhere with us.

Perhaps a better analogy is that some of us have dated debt, some of us are in long term relationships with debt, and many of us have been living in debt so long, we're practically married to it. Freedom can be yours, but you've got to make the decision to divorce debt. You will have to come to the place where you say, *Debt, I'm done with you. You've traveled with me like a bitter old friend. You're like a life-long companion that always drags me down, but today, Debt, I'm done with you.* This decision requires commitment—every day, you'll have renew your vow to divorce your debt. But ultimately, it leads to freedom.

In Proverbs 22:7, we can see God wants us to have no master other than Himself. This is because God knows He is the only one who has our best interests at heart. We know we were instructed to serve God alone, yet when we go into debt, we become slaves to it. If we read between the lines of that verse, we realize God is saying, *I want you serving only Me, but that can't happen as long as you are a slave to debt.*

Our Heavenly Father loves us with an indescribable love, and He has shown us how to be free from debt. As I talk about three ways to discover financial freedom in this chapter, the main thing I want you to see is there's hope for your financial situation. I want you to know God says all things are possible, so even though your finances may seem beyond repair, God's Word says you can achieve financial freedom if you trust Him and follow these steps.

Take Control of Where Your Money Goes

The first step to being free from debt is to *take control of where your money goes.* Do you ever get the feeling that your money sort of just disappears and you don't really know where it all went? Does it sometimes feel like trying to hold water in your hand? For most people, that's the case, but Proverbs 27:23-24 warns against living that way:

> Be sure you know the condition of your flocks, give careful attention to your herds; for riches do not endure forever, and a crown is not secure for all generations.

In ancient times, sheep were income. They were a shepherd's financial stability, so a good shepherd always knew the condition of his flock. Obviously, the majority of people on the planet today don't raise sheep, but the principle still applies. God is saying you need to stay on top of the condition of your finances. This speaks to never letting money come in and go out without having a handle on it. You should know exactly what you're spending your money on, which gives you an idea of what you can *really afford.* Remember, God says, ". . . give *careful* attention to your herds." What I believe God is saying here is we need to develop a budget. Budgeting was not man's idea; God is the original accountant. Let me say it very clearly: *God wants you to create a budget.* The most effective way to pay careful attention to your finances is by creating a family budget that tells you where you are currently, what's coming in, where you're spending your money, and what you plan to spend your money on.

If you don't know where to start, I highly recommend Dave Ramsey's material. You can go to www.daveramsey.com and start there. Dave is one of the best financial teachers in the world, and everything he teaches is based on the Word of God. On his site you'll find all sorts of free tools that can help you create a budget and stick to it. There are tons of testi-monies from folks who used his method of budgeting to free themselves from tens of thousands of dollars of debt.

I also like what pastor and author John Maxwell once said: "A budget is simply telling your money where to go, instead of wondering where it went." Paying careful attention to your finances by creating a budget is the first critical step you need to take to divorce debt.

The Secret to Living Within a Budget

I want to share a secret with you that you may not have heard in other advice on budgeting. Do you want to know how to successfully create a budget and stick to it? The answer is *gratitude*. Living with gratitude for what you have is the key to living within your means. If you're not sure what I mean, think about your prayer life. Is your prayer life simply a list of things you want God to do for you, or are you consistently thankful for what He has done?

You may wonder what gratitude has to do with budgeting. I believe one of the biggest problems with the American debt culture is the idea that we have to keep up with the proverbial Joneses. When we go into debt to keep up appearances rather than only purchasing what we truly need, we develop a sense of entitlement, which is synonymous with pride and ingratitude. That truth may sting a little, but if you allow it to sink in, it can set you free.

Several years ago, I had a close encounter with this type of behavior. My wife was hosting an evening Bible study at our house, so she lovingly told me to take the kids and get out of the house for the evening. I decided to take them to an awesome burger joint called Zesto, on Ponce de Leon Boulevard in Atlanta. The kids were so excited. We ordered a bunch of junk food, and we were having a great time as we sat in our booth joking and laughing and chowing down on our burgers. The door opened, and this homeless man walked in and made a beeline for our table. He said, "Hey, I'm really hungry and I don't have any money. Could you buy me something to eat?"

Moved with compassion, I said, "Yeah, buddy, of course I'll get you something to eat!"

I took out some cash and tried to hand it to him, but he said, "Please, can you go order it for me?" I quickly realized they probably knew him at the restaurant, and he didn't think they would serve him.

So I agreed, and I walked up to the counter wondering what to get the man. Suddenly I saw it! I was not going to go small. No way. I was going to *bless* this guy. I was going to go all out for him! They had a burger that was a triple stacker--three fat patties with the works. I pointed to it and said, "That's what I want!"

I walked back to the booth, handed the guy the number, and told him his order would be up soon. I was looking forward to seeing his face when he saw that monster burger. Eventually, they called his number, and he walked over, grabbed the bag, and looked inside it. He rolled the bag back up, and I wondered if he noticed the size of the burger. He was halfway to the door when he turned and walked over to our table and started cussing me out. "You didn't even buy me fries!" he barked, and then shook his head and walked out.

I couldn't believe it. I started to get angry, but in that moment God whispered in my heart, *What are you getting so mad about? You do that to me all the time.*

Feeling a little hurt, I thought, *What do you mean, Lord?*

You pray, and I'll answer, and your response is "Come on, Lord, you didn't even get me fries with that!"

Boy, that hurt. It was a sort of Heavenly spanking, if you know what I mean.

The point is this: we must never become so spoiled that we expect God to bless us. When we are grateful, it does something to bring us into contentment, and it removes our compulsion to keep up the world's appearances. With gratitude, our focus zeroes in on God's kingdom, and we understand how to use and enjoy what He has given us. Gratitude reduces the temptation to go into debt for foolish reasons.

Be Content Living Within Your Budget

The second step to being free from debt builds on the first one. It is to *be content living within your budget*. Proverbs 21:20 says, "The wise store up choice food and olive oil, but fools gulp theirs down."

The wise person is one who says, "There's not an endless supply here, so I'm going to save a little." He looks to the future, plans ahead, and is happy to limit his consumption. Fools, having no thought for the future, gulp everything down in one day. The wise person knows to live not only below his means and to never over-leverage himself, but to also save for a rainy day. By contrast, the fool consumes more and more and more, until one day he wakes up and he's a *slave*. Another way of saying it is the fool drifts aimlessly, spending paycheck after paycheck, impulsively purchasing stuff he doesn't need to give him a temporary rush, while his bank account is in ruin.

A side effect of this behavior is what I call debt regret, otherwise known as buyer's remorse. Have you ever experienced that? You want something so desperately, and you just know it will make you happy. You can't wait to save for it, so you buy it on the credit card. Before you even finish paying it off, it's gathering dust, not fulfilling you anymore.

One day I experienced something that put this truth in perspective. I was walking in the woods and I looked down to see this weird little bug walking around at my feet. Until that day, I had no idea this particular bug lived in our area, but I knew exactly what it was the moment I saw it. This bug walked up on its front legs, while with its big back legs it pushed around a big ball of stuff it had collected in the woods. It was a dung beetle!

I watched this little beetle start in one spot and push a ball of dung all the way over to another spot. He stopped at that spot for a second, and then he pushed his ball of dung over to another spot. As he pushed it around, collecting bits of dung here and there, his ball grew bigger and bigger. Suddenly, it struck me how many of us are just like that: our whole life consists of pushing a ball of dung to this room, then to the basement, then to the garage, then we'll push it over to a storage unit and lock it away. In fact, did you know that just a couple of years ago, Bloomberg reported that the best real estate investment in the past decade wasn't fancy beach houses or commercial buildings? It wasn't buying a fixer-upper and flipping it, as the infomercials would have you believe. The best real estate investment in the past decade was five-foot-by-five-foot storage lockers.

Smart real estate investors were putting their money in storage units because Americans are addicted to buying stuff and storing it, always hoping our ball of dung is just a little bigger than our neighbor's. Then one day we die and everybody comes in and either divides up our dung or throws it away. And we call that living.

Believe it or not, there is actually a scripture that speaks to this behavior. Philippians 3:8 says, "Yea doubtless, and I count all things but loss for the excellency of the knowledge of Christ Jesus my Lord: for whom I have suffered the loss of all things, and do count them but dung, that I may win Christ." Did you see that? This is the model of contentment for us. Paul considered material things just a ball of dung compared to gaining Christ. So I want to ask, do you find yourself in that trap where you're working so hard, sacrificing all your time trying to get this new car, or a new boat, or eating out all the time? Whatever it is, ultimately it's all dung compared to your calling in Christ. God can make our lives meaningful. He can make them count for His glory and purpose, but He can only do it when we've found contentment in Him and not in the things of this world. Focusing on what really matters, living to impress your Lord, is how you escape the trap of living to impress the world.

Now, I don't want to be too harsh. I know many people start out with the best intentions, especially when they are young or first get married. They strive to be debt-free and are making enough money to buy what they want and maybe even have some left over. Then they have kids. They have to buy cribs, strollers, and a minivan after they pay the hospital bills. They had a great plan, but they got blown off course. It happens all the time, and that's why we need step three.

Save, Give, and Invest for the Future

Once you've taken control of where your money goes and learned to be content living within your budget, the third step to becoming debt-free is much easier to accomplish. In fact, even though you still have to work on it, in time it will become a great joy to you. Step three is *save, give, and invest for the future*. The great thing about this third step is that it is really a payoff for the first two. Divorcing debt makes the future brighter. It seems more secure and hopeful. Suddenly, we have a sense of control over our lives, and we feel good about it. Believe it or not, you'll be so proud of yourself that you'll actually look forward to saving money!

Proverbs 21 says, "The plans of the diligent lead to profit as surely as haste leads to poverty." This is a profound scripture. Notice the noun in that sentence is "plans." What if we substituted the word "budget" for "plans," since a budget is essentially a financial plan? In essence, Solomon is saying a budget is the first step of a financial plan.

Next, notice the word "diligent"; it's a really interesting word. A simple search on Google pulls up this definition: "careful and persistent work or effort." There's that word "careful" again, which is a large part of diligence, and it is coupled with persistence. Simply put, diligence is careful, methodical, persistent work. It leads to profit and abundance.

There is more, though. John Wesley, the great theologian, said it simply but beautifully: "Make all you can, save all you can, and give all you can."

Let's talk about saving. It isn't a difficult concept to grasp, but that doesn't mean it's easy to accomplish. Once you have taken control of your finances with a budget, you will eventually knock out your debt. This is a glorious and deeply liberating experience. You must work for it, and you should celebrate once it happens, but it is not the end of the line. Your next adventure is to start saving for the future. Remember what I said about easily veering off course? Debt is usually just one crisis away, and you never want to end up there again. A good rule of thumb for saving is to work toward maintaining six months of your bills in savings. This is what you should have in liquid cash, available on hand.

While you are saving, or even when you first start budgeting, you may be tempted to cut back on giving to the Lord's work. *Do not do this.* You'll be shutting down many opportunities for the Lord to bless you. I'm not saying if you give to God's work you'll get a certain amount back, but what I am saying is your church does much more for you than you realize. If everyone in your local church neglected to support it, it would close. Churches don't charge for membership, even though they usually do a lot more for you than the restaurants you spend hundreds of dollars a month on, or the gym, or various clubs you belong to. Those activities are good, of course, but without the local church, the world would descend into darkness. The church is the light, and you are responsible, with all your fellow church members, to keep that light shining in your own life and to help keep the lights on in the church. At church, you receive social support, spiritual food, and teaching. You should, in turn, support your local church. If you're not part of a local church, you need to get into a good, Bible-based one. Then find some ministries you resonate with, and give of your time as well.

Beyond the church, find people and families in need. Share with them. Support them with money, clothes, service--whatever they need. Find a single mom who is struggling and help her out. Adopt an elderly widow. This is what the apostle James calls "pure religion" in James 1:27.

Next, you need to earn as much money as you reasonably can. I won't go into great depth on this step, but diligent people are not afraid of working hard, and they capitalize on every opportunity to earn income *without* sacrificing peace of mind. Maybe for a season, if you have time, take an extra job to knock out your debt or help you start to save. Perhaps your hobby can generate some extra money. Maybe have a yard sale, and clear out all that dung you've collected. Find out where you can cut some things you don't need. Remember, a dollar saved is a dollar earned.

Finally, you want to invest for the future. Proverbs 13:22 says, "When a good man dies, he leaves an inheritance to his grandchildren." I can't give advice on how to invest, but I will tell you God intends for us to invest so we can leave something for our children and even our grandchildren. This is only possible once we have taken control of our finances, are living contentedly within our means, and have saved enough to have a cushion in case of emergencies.

Again, I highly recommend visiting Dave Ramsey's website for investment advice. He approaches the topic with much wisdom, yet he never gives personal advice out of his depth. He does, however, have tools to search for Endorsed Local Providers for investing, insurance, real estate, and taxes. Take a look and proceed diligently, with much wisdom.

As we close this chapter, the last thought I want to leave you with is this: God wants you to be free. He never meant for you to be enslaved to debt, yet most of us have made choices that enslave us. There are so many good Christians who are just financially imprisoned. It's so hard for them to serve and so hard for them to give because they are not free. It's hard for them to even function because debt has such a stranglehold on them. I don't want you to be bound like that. I want you to be free.

Today God has given you an option: you can divorce debt. Are you ready to be free? If so, drive that stake in the ground and divorce debt for good. If you do, and you stick to it, it may not be today, it may not be tomorrow, but one day, you will be free of debt. If you follow these principles, you'll have more than enough.

This is a new day for you. Make the decision. Start working on it, and your payoff will arrive sooner than you know.

7

REFUSING TO CONTROL OUR TONGUE

Strong minds discuss ideas,
average minds discuss events,
weak minds discuss people.

--Socrates

Remember the old playground rhyme "Sticks and stones may break my bones, but words will never harm me"?

It's a lie. The older I get, the more I realize how devastating words can be. Words can hurt. In fact, I think words can do more harm than sticks and stones ever could. If I took a survey, I'm sure we would all say we've experienced the pain of destructive words.

That leads us to the sixth stupid thing we do to mess up our lives, which is *refusing to control our tongues.* Now, I used the word *refuse* here on purpose. I realize some of us are tempted to say, "Man, I'd love to control my tongue, but I just simply can't." We even joke about it because being blunt and forthright is appreciated in our culture. We may claim we have no ability to control our tongue, but look at what God's Word says in Proverbs 18:2: "Words kill, words give life; they're either poison or fruit—you choose." Do you see that last word--choose? That is a critical distinction; the Bible says we all have a choice. Words kill or words give life. They're either poison or they're fruit, and it's up to us which they will be.

Most of us only casually consider the words coming from our mouths, and maybe that's because of the sing-song playground rhyme insisting words can never harm us. But if the Bible says our words contain the power of life and death, we should, at the very least, investigate how much damage we could be doing with our tongues. For starters, James 3:4-6 shows us the potentially destructive power of the tongue:

> And a small rudder makes a huge ship turn wherever the pilot chooses to go, even though the winds are strong. In the same way, the tongue is a small thing that makes grand speeches. But a tiny spark can set a great forest on fire. And among all the parts of the body, the tongue is a flame of fire. It is a whole world of wickedness, corrupting your entire body. It can set your whole life on fire, for it is set on fire by hell itself.

Isn't it scary to think your tongue can set your entire life on fire? In addition, it's a double-edged sword: if the tongue has the potential to create life-giving fruit, the opposite is also true. It can kill. I'm reiterating this because I really want you to realize the power words can have.

Here's a slightly different example of how words carry power: I recently received a text from a friend who is a pastor on north side of Atlanta. Every week, he goes to his son's school and offers words of encouragement to his son's football team. My pastor friend was asking me to pray for him because he had received notice of a lawsuit against him. In fact, the school was also named in the lawsuit. His words were meant as encouragement, but because they came from the Bible, someone took offense. That lawsuit alone shows how words carry undeniable power. I understand the argument that sometimes we need to obey God rather than man, but there are also times when we need to use wisdom, and we have to be careful where we place our words. Words can be an incredible tool for God's glory and for His purpose, but we need to use our words to bring life. The fact that my friend's words of Biblical encouragement were attacked on a legal level shows how much the enemy understands the power of our words.

I came across an interesting study the other day. Russian scientists have proven that words can be used to reengineer DNA. That blew my mind. What they've discovered is spoken words can manipulate DNA to the point that something new can be created and/or changed within our DNA. It shouldn't be that surprising, I suppose, because in Genesis 1:3, the Bible tells us God created everything with the spoken word: "Then God said, 'Let there be light,' and there was light."

The first chapter of John plainly tells us God has always spoken everything into existence. If God uses His words as a creative force, and we're made in God's image, do you think maybe we could use our words as a creative force, perhaps actually change the world with our words? Might we be able to speak and create? You see, science is only now catching up with what is already written in God's Word. What's very interesting about this is the Bible talks about using our words creatively in our faith. All throughout the book of Proverbs, we're warned to be careful of the words we speak because those words hold the power of both life and death.

I'm particularly excited about this chapter because, out of all of the stupid things we've talked about in this book, this is the one that can bring instant change in our lives. Words have a tremendous amount of power, and when you harness that power for good, you will see immediate results.

How Words Do Damage

Let's get down to the nuts and bolts of how we misuse our tongues. To make this more engaging, I've come up with a list of character names, but I have a disclaimer: all characters appearing in this work are fictitious, and any resemblance to real persons living or dead is purely coincidental. I promise I'm not talking about you! Your pastor didn't send me a secret note asking if I could use you as an example in my book to teach you a lesson. What will likely happen though, is most of us will recognize these characters. As you read, try not to judge others; instead, see if you recognize yourself in these characters. As we go through the list, ask yourself if you have any of these tendencies.

Gossipy Greta

Gossipy Greta just loves to collect tidbits of information, doesn't she? She's like a kid on Halloween night. "What tasty treat do you have for me?" she asks, licking her lips. Gossip is like a jumbo-sized box of Milk Duds to her--sweet and delicious, and she generously shares with the next person. She doesn't care if these private, slanderous details about other people are accurate or not; they're just too good to keep to herself.

Greta is also slick; she's very, very sneaky in how she shares her gossip. Sometimes she masks it as a prayer request. You know how it goes, right? "I'm really concerned about the Robertson family because they're going through X, Y, and Z. I just know you are concerned, too, so maybe we can all just pray." Yes, she'll stoop that low to disguise her gossip. Her heart is black with malice, but you know who is just as guilty as Gossipy Greta? The person *who listens to her.* The person who wants the dirt on others simply to feel better about his or her own situation.

When you encounter a Gossipy Greta, you must stop her right in her tracks. Shut her down, even publicly. Tell her, "I refuse to gossip. That 'news' is not for me." Because if you don't, you could be her next victim.

Profane Pete

Our next character is *Profane Pete.* If anyone is unable to control his tongue, it's Pete. I saw him just yesterday, as I was driving on the highway. He cut me off and then let the venom spew.

I often meet Pete when couples come into my office for marriage counseling. We'll sit down and begin to share, and Pete's wife will say, "Pastor Beau, you won't believe what he called me," and she whispers some horrible word.

Pete excuses it by saying, "She just brings out the worst in me."

My response is this: "Tomorrow, you when get to work, I want you to walk up to your boss and call him the exact same thing you called your wife."

I am always met with a dumbfounded expression. Pete quickly admits there is no way he'd curse at his boss. What he is really saying is he has a choice. If he can choose not to swear at his boss, he can choose not to swear at his wife. Each and every day, he can choose whether life or death comes out of his mouth.

Watch out for Pete. He'll poison your river.

Negative Ned

Do you ever remember Winnie-the-Pooh's friend Eeyore? No matter what anyone said to Eeyore, he'd always reply with something negative, like, "I'm not much of a donkey." It makes you want to say, "Come on, Eeyore! It's just negative all time." It's the same with Negative Ned; nothing is ever good enough for him. When Ned's daughter gets home from school and says, "Look, Dad! I got an A minus," he responds, "Why didn't you get an A?"

Watch out for Negative Ned. He'll suck the life out of you with his words.

Nagging Nora

Number four is *Nagging Nora*. When I mentioned her at my church, moans rippled throughout the congregation. Proverbs 27:15 compares a nagging spouse to the constant dripping of a faucet. Drip. Drip! DRIP. Could you imagine being married to that? A drip?

I had a friend who was eighty-two years old when his wife passed away, and he had been married to her for over sixty years. One day he said the most incredible thing to me. He whispered, "Beau, I've never done any single thing right in her eyes." My jaw dropped. They were married for over half a century, and to the best of his knowledge, he had never done a thing right. Something was always wrong. I thought that was truly heartbreaking.

Watch out for Nagging Nora. She'll drive you crazy.

Sarcastic Sam

Sarcastic Sam is a classic. You know Sam. He'll use sarcasm to belittle some-one, and his sole motive is to make himself feel better. Sarcastic Sam rolls his eyes and has other little ways of always making you feel stupid.

Sarcastic Sam's words are toxic. Don't even talk to him.

Lying Lao

Then we have *Lying Lao*. Lao is the guy who lies, then needs to cover that lie, so he lies again. Then he is called out on that lie and he tells another. Lao gets caught in this vicious cycle of lying every chance he gets, and before long, even he doesn't know what is the truth.

You can't trust a thing Lying Lao says. It's like pouring water into a bucket full of holes.

Cutting Cathy

Finally, we meet *Cutting Cathy*. Cathy constantly feels the need to say things that cut other people down. She'll say something sharp to her husband. She'll say something bitter to her son, something harsh to her daughter, something rude to her friend. She uses simple but effective ways to cut people down to the size she wants them.

Do you remember the amusement park game called Whac-A-Mole? The little mole head pops up, and you take that plastic hammer and—whack!--you smack that mole down. Then another pops up--whack! The whole game is just about beating those moles down. That's what I picture when I think of Cathy.

Sadly, there are some people who go through life feeling like their call-ing on this planet is to whack other people with their words. The Cutting Cathys of this world will try to excuse their bad behavior by saying, "Well, that's just who I am. At least I'm honest and say what I mean." It is as though cruelty is a badge of honor. But I urge you to give Cutting Cathy a wide berth. She uses her words as a way to control and manipulate every-body around her.

This is not an exhaustive list by any means; there are many more char-acters. There is *Rumor Ramona*; we all know what she does. Or *Screaming*

Sally, who yells at everyone in her house all day long. There is *Never Wrong Neville.* He can never admit when he's wrong. We can go on and on, but I think you get the idea.

If we're honest, we will admit to having at least one of these characters in us. You may have a little Cathy in you, or I may have a bit of Ned in me. But the good news is that God desires to change us. And he can do it right now.

8

REFUSING TO CONTROL OUR TONGUE, PART TWO

A lie will go 'round the world while the truth is pulling its boots on.

--Charles Spurgeon

Now that we know what the problem is, let's figure out how to fix it. How do we go about controlling our tongues? It should come as no surprise by now that we find the solution very clearly laid out in God's Word.

The first step to controlling our tongues is to *assess the damage we've already done*. In the same way an insurance adjuster assesses the damage from a hurricane, God can show us the wreckage we've caused with our tongues. This first step is critical for healing to take place. You may even realize valuable relationships have been wiped away by the force of your untamed tongue. Sometimes we're oblivious, and that is why it is necessary to ask the Lord these questions: Was any of it my fault? Did anything coming out of my mouth contribute to the death of that relationship?

You should always ask God about your home and family. Proverbs talks about those who completely destroy their house with their words, so ask the Lord, *Is that me? Have I torn up my home with my words so that there's not much left?* This is a time to be very honest and assess the damage you've done with your words. Take responsibility for what the Lord shows you, because unless you do that, you cannot move toward healing the situation.

Matthew 12:34 says, ". . . out of the abundance of the heart a mouth speaks." This is important because it means if you are speaking ungodly things, there is a problem with your heart, and it is essential you allow the Lord to deal with it. Have you ever lashed out at someone and then wondered why? When we ask the Lord to help us assess the damage, He will help us look a little deeper and find the heart issue.

Perhaps someone said something hurtful to you years ago, and it caused damage to your heart. That pain took root, and now it's bearing bad fruit for your family and others. Many times I've had people tell me, "Pastor Beau, my dad used to tell me I was stupid and useless all the time." Think about what a deep wound that causes. If that wound is never properly healed, when the stresses of adulthood arise, you end up spewing the exact same hateful things your dad said to you. Sadly, you end up living out exactly what he said you would be. Part of asking God to help you assess the damage is asking Him to show you the roots of the destruction. They may be wounds inflicted by those who were supposed to care for you. I encourage you to take some time and assess both the damage you've had done to you and the damage you've done to others with your words.

Confess Our Failures to God and Those We've Hurt

After we've assessed the damage, the second step to controlling our tongues is *confessing our failures to God and to those we've hurt*. Once we've taken ownership for our part in the damage, confession simply means agreeing with God on that issue. That's all confession is--admitting you were wrong. The good news, according to I John 1:9, is, "If we confess our sins, He is faithful and just to forgive us our sins and to cleanse us from all unrighteousness."

Once we assess the damage and take responsibility, if we simply confess our sins, God will cleanse us. Then He can heal us. He can remove the root of that heart issue once it has been exposed to His healing light.

Did you know that researchers are discovering that light—ultraviolet light, to be specific--has the power to heal? UV light has been used for disinfection for many years, but scientists are now experimenting with using it to stimulate the immune system. In fact, in his book *Into the Light*, Dr. William C. Douglass claims to have seen a "marked reduction in toxic symptoms" of serious infections within twelve to forty-eight hours of treating patients' blood with UV light and re-injecting it into their bodies.

Think about the metaphor of light being used for disinfection and for healing. If we allow God to shine His light on our shortcomings, He will cleanse and heal them.

While we're on the subject of confession, let's see what James 5:16 has to say: "Confess your sins to each other and pray for each other so that you may be healed. The earnest prayer of a righteous person has great power and produces wonderful results." Isn't that something? Scripture tells us when we are consistently righteous in our walk, our prayers that are made in earnest--meaning they are made in sincerity and with zeal--have "great power." That means your prayers will make a tremendous difference. Now, some of us may not believe we are that righteous, but hold up a minute. Do you remember 1 John 1:9? "If we confess our sins, He is faithful and just to forgive us our sins and to cleanse us from all unrighteousness." If we're cleansed from unrighteousness, what does that mean? It means in God's eyes, you are righteous. Now your prayers become effective, powerful tools that will bring healing and hope and will restore relationships. That's really good news.

The key, however, is to confess our sins. It all begins with confession. I suppose the problem is it's not easy to confess. It's easier to live in denial. It's easier to point the finger and put the blame on somebody else. But when we come clean before God and allow Him to point out those areas where we are at fault, it allows repentance from and, therefore, forgiveness of the sin. Our Father can then make us righteous--in "right standing"--with Him. Doesn't that fill you with so much hope?

Once we have confessed our sins to the Lord, we need to confess them to one another. This is another critical step to healing that cannot be ignored. If you were treated unjustly, you would want to be vindicated, right? That is why we need to give those we've wronged that vindication. Only then will God be free to heal us and reward us with restored relationships.

It is hard to confess our sins to one another, but it is the only way to repair damaged relationships. The following are some examples of phrases that can bring tremendous healing into your home. Phrase number one is simply, "I was wrong." Phrase number two: "I'm sorry." Phrase number three: "Will you forgive me?" I highly recommend using these phrases often.

It can be very tough to confess to our friends and fellow church members, but to be honest, I believe it is even harder to confess to our own families. Especially for us dads, right? So often, we men have this mindset that we can never admit to our kids if we are wrong. We figure they might lose respect for us as their father, and besides, we're supposed to know it all. Let me put your heart at rest, dads: your kids are already well aware you don't know it all. And when you are wrong, they know it very well. They're just waiting to hear it from you. Have you ever wondered what would happen if you had the courage to say to your child, "Honey, do you remember the other day when I lost my temper with you? I was completely wrong, and I'm so sorry. Will you forgive me?"

If you had the courage to do that, the respect that child has for you would shoot through the roof. Alternately, if you moms decided to do the tough thing and apologize to your child, you would experience unbelievable healing in that relationship. Where there seemed to be no hope whatsoever, through the words of confession and humility in your mouth, there can be life where there once was only death. There can be fruit where once there was only poison.

Trust me. Confess your mistakes to those you've hurt and watch the miracles take place.

We Meditate On the Word of God

Once we've confessed our sins in obedience, the third step to controlling our tongues is to *meditate on the Word of God*. Psalms 19:14 says, "May the words of my mouth and the meditation of my heart be pleasing to you, O Lord, my rock and my redeemer."

Remember the verse I mentioned earlier that tells us "out of the abundance of the heart the mouth speaks"? What comes out of your mouth is simply the fruit of what you put into your heart.

If you have a child, think back to when he or she was a baby. You'd feed the baby and right afterward, somebody would come along and want to play with the kid. The zealous aunt or uncle or grandma would start tossing that baby in the air, and suddenly the baby threw up on the person. I'm sure you noticed your baby didn't throw up Beef Wellington after you fed her formula or pureed carrots. When babies are shaken, what comes out is what was inside.

In the same way, when we're driving down the highway and someone cuts us off, suddenly all of these words we normally wouldn't say come spewing out of our mouth, and we wonder where on Earth that came from. It came from what was already in our minds and hearts. That has been our diet. What we are watching and what we are hearing is what will come out when we're shaken.

Do you remember the days when you'd see a movie and they'd use a certain curse word and you couldn't believe they used that word? Now you hear that same word a hundred times in a movie, and you don't even notice it until you recommend the movie to your parents! Yet we're still surprised when somebody shakes us up a little, and that word comes out. If we want something better to come out of our mouths, we have to consume something better. So ask yourself right now, what are you consuming day in and day out? Philippians 4:8 says, "Fix your thoughts on what is true, and honorable, and right, and pure, and lovely, and admirable. Think about things that are excellent and worthy of praise."

I was taking a walk in the woods the other day, and my phone dinged to tell me I had a text from my wife. She was at home reading God's Word, and she saw a very tasty scripture--you know, like when you have to share a piece of a delicious steak at a restaurant—and the first thing she thought was, "I need to share this with my husband!" She was asking what I thought about this verse. Her heart's meditation was shared with me, which caused me to begin meditating on pure and lovely things--things admirable and excellent and worthy of praise. And guess what? The next time either of us is shaken up, the next time we're frustrated or angry or stressed out about something, instead of garbage, what will come out? God's Word will come out. Out of the abundance of those good and lovely and admirable things in our hearts will flow good and admirable and lovely things from our mouths. Once you've started meditating on what is good, someone might ask you, "Wow, where did that wisdom come from?"

You can respond, "Well, I just meditated on it from the Word of God earlier. It's part of my diet, part of the meditation of my heart.

That's how you begin to change the world with your words. You'll see your relationships begin to change. You'll see your circumstance change. You'll see everything begin to change.

We Purpose to Bless Others With Our Words

The fourth and final step to controlling our tongues is *purposing to bless others with our words.* Remember, we have a choice in everything we say, but when we're shaken, what is in our hearts will come out. There is another way, though, in which we can train ourselves to tame our tongues and use them for good: we can purpose to bless others with our words. Ephesians 4:29 says, "Watch the way you talk. Let nothing foul or dirty come out of your mouth. Say only what helps, each word a gift."

If each word is a gift, consider what you are giving your children. What are you giving your spouse? What are you giving to those who you work with you every day? Are you feeding people poison, or are you giving them the bread of life? What is coming out of your mouth--words that bring life or words that bring death?

When I was still in college, a pastor asked my friend and me if we'd mind teaching a Sunday school class. I didn't know much about teaching Sunday school, but I wanted to do whatever I could to help out around the church, so I figured, Why not? Once I'd agreed, my pastor added, "By the way, you're going to be teaching fifth-grade boys!" Whoa, I thought, fifth-grade boys? I decided we'd do what we could.

On the first day, thirty fifth-grade boys came tumbling into the classroom. You can just imagine; they were rowdy and wild and running and jumping all over the place. So we were trying to wrangle them, and we finally got them to calm down and sit in their chairs--well, all of them except for one boy. This boy's name was John, but we called him Little John because his dad was Big John. When Little John came into the class, I'd never seen anything like it before. Little John had more anger and rage than anyone I've ever seen in my life, even to this day. He walked into the class and immediately went over to one of the school desks and launched it across the room, almost seriously injuring some of the other boys. My jaw dropped. I mean, who expects a kid to do that? Then he walked over to a chair, so my buddy and I started trying to shield the boys in front of him, as I half-yelled, "Little John, what are you doing? You'd better sit down!"

He didn't sit down. He grabbed a chair and hurled it across the room. Needless to say, I knew we weren't going to be able to restrain this kid without a physical confrontation, so I went to the auditorium and found Big John and told him what was going on with his son. With a grim look on his face, Big John said, "Don't worry, I'll take care of it." He marched back to the class and pulled Little John out into the hallway, slamming the door behind them. Suddenly, we heard the most obscene profanities and brutal words spewing out of Big John's mouth from the other side of the door. Everyone in the room just sat there in shock. I couldn't believe what I was hearing. Of course, the more I heard coming out of Big John's mouth, I started to realize why Little John behaved the way he did. But I now had an even bigger problem because I had no clue how to handle the situation.

Eventually, the door flew open, and Little John slunk back into the room as Big John glared over his shoulder. Big John nodded to me, and I kind of nodded back like, "Wow! Uh, thanks?" Big John headed back to church. With pure rage in his eyes, Little John walked right over to another chair and flung it across the room. I knew I wasn't going to ask Big John for help again, but I had no idea what else I could do.

For several days, I was at a loss about what to do. I went to my mom and asked her advice, and she had no idea, but she told me my grandmother, who had been a preschool teacher for years before she retired, was really good at stuff like that. So I went to my grandma's house. I explained the whole situation to her and told her I had no clue how to handle it.

Grandmom narrowed her eyes a little, but she sat in her chair, silent, for a bit.

Finally, she spoke. "Next Sunday, I want you to take a jar full of candy to the class."

"Okay. I think I know where you're going with this." I figured she wanted me to try to bribe Little John.

"At the beginning of class," Grandmom continued, "announce to all the boys that jar of candy is going to the best behaved kid in the class that day."

"Okay," I said, following her, certain this plan wouldn't help Little John.

"At the end of class," she said, "stand up and make a big deal out of the ceremony. Then you announce, 'Today, the best kid in class is . . . LITTLE JOHN!'"

"Grandmom, I don't think you understand. He's not the best kid. He's completely out of control."

Grandmom just nodded and said, "I know. Just try it and see what happens."

"Okay," I agreed, shrugging my shoulders, "I'll give it a try." I didn't have a better idea.

That next Sunday, I went to class armed with my jar of candy. All of the boys were there, and once again, Little John was acting crazy, throwing stuff around the room. I went to the front and held up the jar of candy and said, "Listen up, guys! Today I have this jar of candy." That got their attention. Even Little John stopped knocking over a pile of books to eye the tempting jar. "This jar of candy is going to go the most well-behaved kid in the class today," I said. All the boys' eyes got big. They began acting as if they'd been little angels the entire time. Well, all of them except for Little John. As soon as he heard the terms, his eyes fell, and he looked away.

For the rest of the class, all of the boys were on their best behavior, each trying to outdo the rest. But Little John was exactly the same. He threw more stuff around, wouldn't stop talking during the lesson, and he generally just acted rowdy. When we finally reached the end of the class,

I knew who would get the jar of candy, but I thought to myself, I can't believe I'm going to go through with this.

"All right, all right, simmer down," I chided, as the boys all chattered excitedly. I could see each one wondering if he would win the candy.

"Everybody listen up," I said as seriously as I could. "I'm going to give away the jar of candy to the boy who really tried the hardest to be on his best behavior in class today."

They all held their breath. "The jar of candy goes to . . ."

All of their eyes were big as they sat straight up in their desks. Except Little John. He had his head on his arms, lying on his desk.

"The best kid in the class today is . . . LITTLE JOHN!"

Every other boy in the class looked at me like, "Whaaaat?" but Little John sat bolt upright in his desk with a confused look on his face. I said, "Little John, come on down and pick up your prize, buddy." Skeptical, he slowly got up out of his seat, but I could see a light of hope flickering faintly in his eyes. He trudged to the front with a frown, but when I handed him his prize, he looked up at me and politely said, "Thank you." All the boys were dumbfounded, but I was already astounded by what was taking place, and I couldn't wait for the following Sunday.

The next Sunday, Little John came back to class. He didn't launch any desks at the other boys. He didn't hurl any chairs at the wall. Do you know who the best kid in the class was that Sunday and every Sunday after that? Little John. Do you know why? Because somebody spoke words of life over him, telling him he was the best-behaved kid in class. That was something he had never heard before. Somebody spoke life where, before, all Little John heard was death. This is true of every single one of us. God has spoken life over you, but you can either purpose to bless others with your words, or curse them. Poison or fruit? You get to choose.

As I close this chapter, I thought it only appropriate to do something that God commanded the children of Israel to do every day. Each day the people would come before Aaron, the first high priest of Israel. Aaron would stand up with his hands outstretched over the people and speak the words below. I would like to do the same over you, your family, and your loved ones. Think about each word and receive it over your life. Then go out and live that word. These words are not my words. They are the words God, your Father, is speaking over your life.

> The Lord bless you and keep you;
> The Lord make His face shine upon you,
> And be gracious to you;
> The Lord lift up His countenance upon you,
> And give you peace (Numbers 6:24-26).

I think we need those words spoken over us every day. What you might not realize is Jesus, your great high priest, speaks those words over you every single day. He is your intercessor in Heaven. Because of Him, you have God's grace. You have God's peace. You have God's favor in your life. You've been blessed by God.

That is why you can go and bless others in the same way.

9

FAILING TO CONTROL OUR ANGER

Anger is an acid that can do more harm to the vessel in which it
is stored
than to anything on which it is poured.

--Mark Twain

Our final chapter is about the thing that has the potential to do the most damage in our lives. It is also the trickiest stupid thing in the book because there is a righteous version of it. The key to discerning the difference, of course, is relying on your relationship with the Lord in your daily walk. So let's get into it. I believe anyone reading this would agree we all suffer from stupid thing number seven, *failing to control our anger*.

Proverbs 14:2 says, "People with understanding control their anger; a hot temper shows great foolishness." Be honest; would you say there have been instances where you have shown great foolishness when you were angry? I think we can all say yes, and we can all relate to the damage anger can do.

Not long ago, I was driving on Interstate 75 near Atlanta with my wife. I was in the far right lane, doing at least the speed limit. I was cruising along at a pretty good little clip when I glanced in my rear-view mirror and all I could see was the grill of a huge truck right up on me. I mean, he was almost touching my rear bumper, really trying to push me. A feeling of anxiety immediately rushed through me, but I was in the slowest lane already, so I couldn't move over. In addition, I was already going pretty fast, so I didn't need to speed up. I continued along at my normal speed, but the longer we went, the more upset I became.

Then things started racing through my head like, *What's this guy's malfunction? He's endangering my wife and me.* I started getting angry. Eventually, he whipped out to go around me on the left, but he was so close he almost clipped my rear bumper. By that point, I was getting really mad. He drove up alongside me and turned his blinker on. *Oh no, you don't,* I thought. *If you're going to be that way, then I'm gonna do this,* and I sped up a little. He sped up, but I acted like I didn't see him, and I sped up. He slowed down again, so I slowed down. I have to admit I thought to myself, *I'm just playing the game you started, man.*

Of course, my wife was starting to get nervous, and she said, "Stop it, Beau!"

I looked at her, the picture of innocence, and said, "What? I don't know what you're talking about."

She obviously knows me better than anyone, so she raised her voice, "Stop it now, Beau! Just quit!"

I just shrugged in confusion, but I continued to play my game with the truck for a little while, not letting him pass or get back behind me. You see, I had some deep anger that had to be released at that point, so I just kept on. After a while, satisfied that had I taught the guy a lesson, I slowed down and allowed him to whip around in front of me and keep driving.

I gave my wife a smug grin, and she said, "You know you missed our exit, right?" Because of my anger, I had to drive an extra fifteen miles just to get to where we were going.

I really don't like that about myself. I don't like how sometimes something gets hold of me and it feels like I can't control the rage. In fact, it feels like anger completely grabs control of me. It's a Jekyll-and-Hyde type of thing where I want to be patient and longsuffering, but suddenly, some weird monster comes out and I start behaving like a heathen.

That story may have you chuckling a bit, as I'm sure many of you can relate, but in the grand scheme of things, driving fifteen extra miles is not that big of a deal. But broken homes are a big deal. Failed marriages, lost jobs, physical sickness, domestic abuse--these things are very big deals. The truth is, if you give anger an inch, it will begin to take a mile. It is one of the most dangerous traits you can allow in your life, and the reason is, we often have valid reasons to justify it.

We need to control our anger, but how? As always, God has a solution. The Word of God gives us five ways to control our anger and keep from messing up our lives.

The first thing we need to do is open our hearts. Years ago, on my very first Sunday as pastor at my home church, I gave a message on this topic. As I began to talk, a man in the audience realized I was preaching about anger, and he actually got it into his head that his wife had called me in advance and asked me to preach that message just for him. It angered him that I was talking about anger. In fact, it angered him so much he and his wife walked out of the service. On their way out, one of our church staff members asked him if everything was okay, and he told the staff member they were leaving because I was talking about him. Isn't that the saddest thing? I'm sure God's Spirit wanted to do something in that man's life. He needed that message the most, and God had him there to bring healing to his life. But he refused to hear it.

What I am trying to say is, especially if this is touching a nerve, God has you reading this chapter for a reason. Will you open your heart and allow Him to minister to you? Don't you want to be free of slavery to anger?

Resolve To Control Your Anger

The first step to controlling anger is *resolving to control it*. This is a deliberate choice. It is reaching the place where you say, "Lord, I need help." When you reach that place, it opens the door for Him to work on those areas. Proverbs 29:11 says, "Fools vent their anger, but the wise quietly hold it back."

God is saying wise people hold back from venting their anger (as you'll see, this is not the same thing as pushing it down or denying it). This means having the wisdom not to fly off the handle when you get angry. You may be wondering where to get that kind of wisdom. I have good news for you! If you need God's help to make some changes, and if you have the desire to change, He is ready to help. It's right there in James 1:5: "If you need wisdom, ask our generous God, and he will give it to you. He will not rebuke you for asking."

How great is that? God won't be mad at you for asking. He knows you need help. Too often, however, we tend to think to ourselves, "I don't have everything together in my life. I've made a mistake here and I've messed up there. Certainly God doesn't feel like helping me." So, we stay away from Him, effectively standing off from our Father. We tend to believe He'll start helping us when we get our act together, but that's the exact opposite of what God has said in His Word. He offers to give us wisdom generously, but you have to be at that place where you are ready to receive His help.

Resolving to control our anger is the beginning. From there, we ask the Lord for wisdom. We have to come a place of humility first, and then God can begin to work. Some of us, however, will ask God for His help, but then we don't take the necessary steps when He shows us what to do. You have to follow through in faith. God will give you wisdom if you commit to doing what you can. When you have reached the end of your power, that's when God takes over. So resolve to control your anger, and ask the Lord for the wisdom to do it. That's the first step.

Realize the Cost of Anger

The second step to controlling anger is *realizing what that anger costs*. Proverbs 29:22 says, "An angry person starts fights; a hot-tempered person commits all kinds of sin." Proverbs 14:17 says, "Short-tempered people do foolish things, and schemers are hated."

These scriptures are pretty straightforward in that they show us there are sinful and foolish consequences for anger. What are they? Well, I'd like to tell you about a member of our congregation named Vince. When

Vince gave his testimony at our church, he introduced himself by saying, "My name is Vince, and I'm a child of God who is in recovery. I struggle with anger." This is Vince's testimony:

> Saying I struggle with anger is giving anger a bad name. After all, anger's a God-given emotion, and it's okay to get angry over something from time to time. But what I suffered with is a short temper followed by rage. At my worst, during a bout of road rage, I would chase people down just to let them know how I felt. How's that for insanity?
>
> My life started changing nine years ago this coming March. I was lying in the Intensive Care Unit of Emory University Hospital in Midtown, recovering from open-heart surgery. A quadruple bypass. My doctors told me part of the cause was poor lifestyle choices but the main reason was stress. Earlier the morning of my heart attack, I flew into a rage over a business deal that went sour. The doctors thought that was probably what triggered the attack.
>
> Looking back in my life, I was always an angry kid. I think this was partly because of my situation at home. I was born to loving parents, but we lived in a three-flat apartment building owned by my grandfather. My grandfather was from Sicily, the home of the mafia, and I'm not saying that he was in the mafia, but he ran the house like he was. He was the head of the family.
>
> As a kid, it was a constant battle between trying to do what my parents wanted me to do and doing what my grandfather told me to do. I would sneak around the house most of the time, trying to avoid my grandfather. When he caught me, he would assign me some chore to do around the building, but when I finished it, it never seemed to be to his satisfaction. This behavior was a major source of frustration for me and also gave me a feeling that I was not good enough. Of course, I would take this frustration out

on the other kids in the neighborhood. I wasn't a bully, but everyone knew not to make me angry because I had a short fuse. Which in itself was a source of frustration. I didn't want to be that kid. I wanted everyone to like me.

My grandfather's behavior continued into my early teen years when my father died. That was when I was a junior in high school. My grandfather was now running the show, and things only got worse. Eventually, my mother, my sister, and I moved away after I graduated high school. But the damage was done. All during my adult years, I struggled with a short temper and rage. It has cost me jobs, relationships--both personal and professional--and most of all, my health.

On March 14, 2006, the night before my surgery, my surgeon came in and he said, "Vince, if you were a younger man, I'd put you on the list for a complete heart transplant. But since you're not, I'm going to go in there tomorrow morning and do the best I can with what I have to work with." That night is when I stopped sweating the small stuff.

In October 2006, we were training to start Celebrate Recovery at Community Bible Church. In January of 2007, I started my first Twelve-Step study. The most profound steps for me were steps four and step five, the inventory steps. They would change my life forever.

In step four, we made a fearless moral inventory of ourselves. The corresponding Bible verse is, "Instead, let us test and examine our ways. Let us turn back to the Lord," from Lamentations 3:40. In step five we admitted to God, to ourselves, and to another human being the exact nature of our wrongs. The corresponding Bible verse is, "Confess your sins to each other and pray for each other so that you may be healed . . .," from James 5:16.

In working through these two steps, I found out that my temper and my rage is my sin, not my character defect. My character defect is, or was, very low self-esteem. I learned that if I wanted to control my anger and rage, with God's help, I first had to work on my low self-esteem. Working through these steps is the hardest work I've ever done. Thanks to that, coupled with a strong accountability team and a strong sponsor, I've had six years of sobriety from that hell called rage.

I always introduce myself the same way, "Hello, my name is Vince. I am a child of God, and I struggle with anger." Well, one night, after a recovery meeting, a regular attendee came up to me and said, "You know, Vince, you always say that you struggle with anger, but I just don't see it." That was the kindest thing anyone could ever say to me. Praise the Lord.

As we can see plainly from Vince's powerful testimony, anger is costly. The price tag attached could be so many things--divorce, violence, injury, death, disease, broken homes, broken relationships, job loss, and the list goes on and on. Notice that most anger affects the nuclear family, and consider these statistics:

- One in every four women will experience domestic violence in her lifetime.
- An estimated 1.3 million women in America are victims of physical assault by an intimate partner each year.
- Eighty-five percent of domestic violence victims are women.
- Historically, females are most often victimized by someone they know.
- Females twenty to twenty-four years of age are at the greatest risk of non-fatal intimate partner violence.
- Most cases of domestic violence are never reported to the police.

(I'll say one thing in regard to these statistics: if you ever want to see some crazy anger, lay a hand on a man's daughter. I know fathers of girls understand where that comes from).

Now, something else we have to consider is we have a Heavenly Father who cares about each and every one of us. So think about what a scary place that is if you are an abuser, if you are somebody who takes out your anger on a child of God. Can you imagine the anger of God? Can you imagine the Father, when He has had enough of somebody hurting his little girl, or his little boy? What a scary place to be. So that is another side of the coin. And it is another one of the costs of anger.

Reflect Before Reacting

The third way to control anger is to *reflect before reacting.* Proverbs 19:11 says, "Sensible people control their temper; they earn respect by overlooking wrongs."

This one is a little trickier to understand, so let's think about what we mean by reflection. To reflect means to take a step back and examine what is causing you to be angry. There is tremendous value in doing this, even beyond controlling your anger. You see, discovering the source of your anger will bring healing in many other areas of your life as well.

I'm going to give you the answer to the test right now. There are three root causes for anger in your life. The first is hurt. The second is fear. The third is frustration. We've all been hurt before, some of us to a greater degree than others. You may have suffered through severe emotional and physical pain in childhood that is now causing anger in your life. You then became the person who passed it on from generation to generation. The good news is it can stop with you, but you must examine your heart deeply to find the hurt that is at the root of your anger. It won't be easy, but it will be liberating. When you find that root, you will very likely have to completely forgive some people, erasing their debt to you. When you do this, you allow God to work, and He will heal you of your hurt, your anger, and all of their consequences.

Maybe fear is causing the anger in your life. Next time you get upset and fly into a rage, take a step back and check to see if you are actually afraid of something. Maybe you're afraid of losing control? Maybe you're afraid of losing security? Whatever it is, take a step back and ask, "Why is it that I am angry?" When you can pinpoint that fear in your life, you can go to the Lord and realize there is no fear in Him, only perfect love. And God's perfect love casts out all fear. You don't have to live in fear any longer. Take the time to examine and recognize that fear today, take it to the Lord as a root of your anger, and allow Him to heal you.

Maybe frustration is causing your anger. Only when you take a step back and reflect, can you see how this scripture applies to you: "Sensible people control their temper; they earn respect by overlooking wrongs." Overlooking wrongs is part of the reflection that has to take place. People will wrong you. People will wrong you every single day. But guess what? You will wrong people every single day, too. At some point, someone has to be the person who starts overlooking the wrongs and forgiving others. Don't you want to be that bigger person? Remember, Jesus sets the example. He knows your wrongs. He knows your sin, but He forgives you, and He takes it all on Himself.

Colossians 3:13 says, "Make allowance for each other's faults, and forgive anyone who offends you. Remember, the Lord forgave you, so you must forgive others." This is a significant part of reflecting. If you stop, breathe, and consider that you have been forgiven for so many things, you'll wonder why you are getting so frustrated with someone else. When you reflect, you're able to see why anger shouldn't control you. You're able to change your perspective.

I heard about a guy who moved his business to a new location, and his wife sent him some flowers to celebrate. When the guy received the flowers, however, the card read, "Rest in peace." They had obviously mixed up his flowers with ones intended for a funeral. The man was trying hard to have a perfect launch, and this really upset him. In anger, he called the flower shop and gave them a piece of his mind. The lady on the other end of the line calmly replied, "Sir, I understand your frustration, but do me a favor. Just for a second, I want you to think that right about now, there is a funeral taking place. The family is in mourning, and our delivery van just showed up with lovely bouquet of flowers and a card that reads, "Congratulations on your new location!""

Perspective makes a world of difference, and you can only see a new perspective when you take time to reflect.

Release Anger Appropriately

The fourth way you control your anger is to *release it appropriately*. This is something most people fail to do, but learning how to do it the right way will change your life faster than anything. Ephesians 4:26 says, "Don't sin by letting anger control you. Don't let the sun go down while you are still angry, for anger gives a foothold to the devil."

Notice the apostle Paul doesn't say, "Don't sin by being angry." He says, "Don't sin by *letting anger control you* (emphasis added). Do you remember at the beginning of the chapter where we read in Proverbs 14:2, "People with understanding control their anger"? This is the flip side of that coin. There is a way to control our anger instead of allowing it to control us.

If you continue reading after Ephesians 4:26, you'll see the apostle Paul describes a transformation process. We'll pick up the passage in verses 31-32: "Get rid of all bitterness, rage, anger, harsh words, and slander, as well as all types of evil behavior. Instead, be kind to each other, tenderhearted, forgiving one another, just as God through Christ has forgiven you."

Can you see the transformation taking place in this scripture? First was the instruction not to sin by allowing anger to control you. One of the Apostle Paul's implications here is even if you have a legitimate reason to be angry, that anger can become a terrible master if it causes you to sin. So how do we get to the place where we have control over anger and the temptation it brings? Well, there has to be this transformation taking place, and the transformation, as always, comes through our relationship with Jesus Christ. As that happens, we learn how to handle our anger.

Four Keys to Releasing Anger Appropriately

It's important not to suppress the anger by denying it's even there. Have you ever been involved in an argument that went something like this:

"Don't be angry!"

"I'm NOT angry!"

That's denial, and it doesn't work.

Second, handling anger appropriately means not repressing it. We repress anger by pushing it down and bottling it up. Some of us are experts at this. We get angry, but nobody knows, and we just shove it deep down in our heart and hold a bitter grudge against the person. We keep tamping it down, and tamping and tamping it down until one day--BOOM! We explode. The scripture says we must get rid of that bitterness, rage, and anger because stuffing it deep inside is how it begins to take root.

Now, it's one thing to not suppress or repress anger, but it is also critical that we don't express anger in the wrong way. Some of us don't struggle with repressing our anger. Oh, no, we erupt like a volcano when something doesn't go our way. That's simply manipulation, and it's a sin. In other cases, we express our anger by making snide comments or taking sarcastic little jabs. Instead, we must express anger in the right way. But how do we do that?

The right way to express anger is to confess it. Before you react, acknowledge your anger and talk to the Lord first. Tell Him you're angry. He's not surprised; in fact, He knows it already. He created you with that emotion, but He does expect you to rely on His Spirit to release your anger appropriately. Also, when you confess to the Lord, an interesting thing happens--you automatically reflect before reacting. Going back to the previous section, you must also ask yourself, "What's really going on here? Am I feeling fear, hurt, or frustration?"

After confessing the anger to the Lord, if you are still struggling to release it, confess the anger to somebody else. Now, I don't recommend confessing it to the person you're angry with, so find a trusted, mature confidant and confess your anger to that person. He or she can help you reflect on it, and release it appropriately.

You might be thinking, What about righteous anger? Is there such a thing, and if so, what would righteous anger look like?

Righteous anger definitely exists. In John 2:14-16, Jesus displayed righteous anger when he drove the money changers out of the temple. Righteous anger is realizing something is blatantly unjust or flagrantly sinful, and it stirs up something in us that wants to make a change for the good. But Jesus expressed the anger, made the change, and then He let it go. It never became anything personal. Remember Ephesians 4:26, which says, "Don't let your anger control you." That's the key.

Watch the news tonight, and you will be stirred with righteous anger at what's going on in the world today. Maybe righteous anger moves you to vote, or fund a campaign, or help clean a stranger's house. Do you have any righteous anger? You should. Too often, we're asleep at the wheel, watching Satan attack our homes, our families, and our nation. We need some righteous anger where we say, "Satan, I've had enough. You're not messing with my kids. You're not messing with my family. You're not messing with my home!" That is the kind of anger God is able to use to do something good and right and profitable. But even with righteous anger, we need to release it appropriately.

Re-Pattern My Mind

Finally--and this key has the potential to completely free you from anger if you apply it--the fifth way to control your anger is to *re-pattern your mind*. It's learning to think in a new way, and it will change your entire life. With the Lord's help, you can change your natural reaction. He can transform you and bring healing into your life just as He brought healing into Vince's life. Your home can be made whole, your relationships can be restored, and you can find the life God has intended for you. But it comes back to that relationship with Jesus Christ.

So what is the primary way we build our relationship with Christ? The Word of God. That is always our foundation and our bedrock. It should come as no surprise that scripture gives us very specific instructions on re-patterning--or renewing--our minds. Take a look at Romans 12:2: "Don't copy the behavior and customs of this world, but let God transform you into a new person by changing the way you think. Then you will learn to know God's will for you, which is good and pleasing and perfect."

Isn't that powerful? What that scripture is saying is changing the way you think has the potential to save you from temptation and to change your entire life. This scripture also relates to Ephesians 4, which tells us to "Get rid of all bitterness, rage, anger, harsh words, and slander, as well as all types of evil behavior. Instead, be kind to each other, tenderhearted, forgiving one another, just as God through Christ has forgiven you."

How do we get rid of all anger, rage, and other such sins? By simply being kind to one another and forgiving each other. How do we do that consistently? We change the way we think by the Word of God. If you look closely, you can see all of the material we've been talking about in this chapter summarized in this verse.

Friend, this is how you overcome anger for good. If you practice the following verse, you will re-pattern your mind, which in turn will help you easily accomplish all of the previous steps in this chapter. Philippians 4:8-9 tells us how to receive the peace of God, which is the opposite of anger:

> And now, dear brothers and sisters, one final thing. Fix your thoughts on what is true, and honorable, and right, and pure, and lovely, and admirable. Think about things that are excellent and worthy of praise. Keep putting into practice all you learned and received from me—everything you heard from me and saw me doing. Then the God of peace will be with you.

Wow! Isn't that so simple? This is how you re-pattern your mind. You consistently think on these good things in the Word, or meditate on them. Memorize them, ponder them, and mull over their meaning. Let them sink into your spirit.

My sister lives in Florida, and she has a lemon tree in her yard. Every fall, it's loaded with lemons the size of softballs, so many she has to give some away. When she comes to visit, she brings Kim a bag full of them. Do you know that not once has Kim ever cut into one of those Meyer lemons and squeezed it and gotten orange juice? What comes out of those lemons is lemon juice because that's what is inside them. In the same way, your mind will produce what you put in it. If what you've put in is God's word, then when you're squeezed, you will be exhibiting things that are true, honorable, lovely, right, and admirable.

10

CLOSING WORDS

Everything happens for a reason.
Sometimes the reason is you're stupid
and you make bad decisions.

— Bill Murray

In early 2015, our church mailed thousands of informational flyers about our services to several communities around our satellite campuses. A young lady found the flyer in her mail and immediately decided she wanted to visit our church, but when her boyfriend saw her reading the flyer, it upset him. Then, when he asked her if she wanted to go to church and she confirmed she did, he flew into a rage and beat the living daylights out of her.

For that young lady, that was it. She had been beaten to a pulp for wanting to attend church and get her life right with God, and that was the last straw. She resolved that day to do something about her situation. This was not the first time her boyfriend had been abusive, but this was the day she did something about it. She called the police, and they rescued her.

That young lady was determined to never return to the foolishness of accepting abuse at the hands of a man, someone who was clearly displaying several of these seven stupid things himself. One thing this young lady did was visit our church. She came that very first Sunday after receiving the flyer in the mail. On that day, she met Jesus, received Him as her Savior, and became a brand new person. She was finally truly free.

I tell you that story because in Jesus Christ, there is always hope. Always. You can avoid these Seven Stupid Things. But there is only one way to truly put these things behind you: you must make a firm decision. You must say, "Enough is enough."

The devil is a bully. He wants to keep smacking you around. He also wants you to maintain a relationship with foolishness. We're all victims to it, and we all escape the same way. We have to make a decision and turn to God for help. In the last chapter, we learned He gives wisdom generously to those who ask for it. You can be free, and once you are, you'll never look back.

Most importantly, I pray as you close this book that you have the very same hope. No matter who you are, no matter where you've been, no matter what struggles you've faced, Jesus Christ adores you, and He wants to heal you today. But you have to allow Him to. He's a gentleman. Unlike your enemy, the devil, Jesus won't try to force you to do anything you don't want to do.

Do you know Jesus? I don't mean know about Him; I mean really know Him, like you know your best friend. If you don't, you can. Romans 10:9 says, "If you confess with your mouth the Lord Jesus and believe in your heart that God has raised Him from the dead, you will be saved."

Jesus is alive and well, and He's actually praying for you right now in Heaven. In fact, I would say the reason you're reading this book is because of God's divine intervention in your life. You can make the decision to call out to Him right now, and begin a new life. If you truly believe that Jesus sacrificed His life on Earth to pay for our foolishness, then rose from the dead by the power of God, and you want to make Jesus Lord over your life, committing the rest of your days to the most wonderful relationship with Him, simply pray the following prayer.

> Dear God in Heaven, I come to you in the name of your son, Jesus. First, I acknowledge my foolishness. I am a sinner, and I want to be free from that sin.
>
> I believe that your Son, Jesus Christ, shed His precious blood on the cross at Calvary to pay for my sins. Today, I say enough is enough. I make the decision to turn my back on my sin, and I commit this day to living the rest of my life for You. Please forgive me of my sins, and make my spirit alive again.
>
> You said in Romans 10:9 that if we confess the Lord our God and believe in our hearts that You raised Jesus from the dead, we will be saved. Right now, I confess Jesus as the Lord of my life. This very moment, I accept Jesus Christ as my own personal Savior, and commit my life to God.
>
> Thank you for your unlimited mercy and grace, which has saved me from my sins. Thank you that your grace never leads to license, but rather it always leads to repentance. Please transform my life through Your Holy Spirit so that I may bring glory and honor to You and never to myself.
>
> According to the promise in Romans 10:9, I am confident right now that I am saved.
>
> Thank you, Jesus, for dying for me and giving me eternal life. I love and worship You. Amen.

Friend, if you prayed that prayer in sincerity, you're saved.

I know your entire world seems brighter, and the burden of sin (foolishness) is gone from your shoulders. You just made the best decision of your life. Please find a good church home in your area, one that follows sound teaching and doctrine, and begin to grow in God. You may face some challenges, but now you have the King of Kings right there with you. You have His Holy Spirit leading and guiding you every step of the way, when you grow to know Him more and more.

Father, thank You so much for this precious person who read this book and made this choice right here, right now, today. Thank You for the life You give us. Thank You for being concerned about us, even in the little things of our daily lives. Thank You that we don't have to remain enslaved to foolishness; instead, You liberate us and You change us when we call out to You. Lord, I pray Your perfect will is done in each and every one of our lives. In Jesus' name I pray. Amen.

ACKNOWLEDGEMENTS

To my Lord and Savior Jesus Christ for everything...
To my wife, Kim, and my kids, Chase and Madison, for your endless love, encourage-
ment, and belief in me as a husband and a father...
To the Community staff and congregation for allowing me to be your friend and pastor
for so many years...
To my sister and writer, Sandi, for encouragement, guidance,
and making me sound smarter than I really am...
With everything in me, I say thank you.

Beau Adams is the pastor of Community Bible Church in Stockbridge, Georgia. With a membership of over 6,000, the church has been on *Outreach* magazine's list of 100 Fastest Growing Churches in America several times in the past decade. With its online campus and multiple locations, Community reaches a global audience every week.

Beau is also affiliated with Dr. John Maxwell's EQUIP Ministries, an organization that sends pastors abroad to train other pastors and leaders. Through EQUIP, he has spoken to large crowds of people in Brazil, Portugal, England, and India.

He holds a BA in Communications from Georgia State University, a MDiv from New Orleans Baptist Theological Seminary, and a PhD in Organizational Leadership from the University of Phoenix.